Rice, Pasta and Eggs

micro wave

Madame Benoit

Encyclopedia of microwave cooking

Rice, Pasta and Eggs

micro wave

Héritage+plus

Données de catalogage avant publication (Canada)

Benoît, Jehane, 1904-

  Rice, Pastas and eggs

  (Héritage+plus) (Encyclopedia of microwave cooking ; 7)
  Issued also in French under title: Pâtes alimentaires,
riz et oeufs.
  Includes index.

  2-7625-5815-8

  1. Cookery (Macaroni). 2. Cookery (Rice). 3. Cookery (Beans). 4. Microwave cookery. I. Title. II. Se-
ries : Encyclopedia of microwave cooking ; 7.

TX832.B4613 1986   641.8'22   C86-096486-8

Front cover design: Bouvry Designer Inc.
Front cover and inside photography: Paul Casavant
Conception and research: Marie-Christine Payette
Cover : Year-round Tomato Sauce

Legal Deposit: first quarter 1987
Bibliothèque nationale du Québec
Bibliothèque nationale du Canada

ISBN : 2-7625-5815-8   Printed in Canada

LES ÉDITIONS HÉRITAGE INC.
300, Arran, Saint-Lambert, Québec J4R 1K5
(514) 672-6710

Table of Contents

Foreword

Over the last twelve years I have watched the fantastic and astonishing progress of the microwave oven. I remain convinced that it is the most effective **stove** we have yet to see in our kitchens. It is efficient, flexible, easy to clean, takes little space compared to all other types of stoves. To start cooking, it need only be plugged in like a toaster. Food cooks in a mini length of time, but speed isn't its only plus. It also features variable power, automatic **defrost** and **defrost cook.** Above all, remember it will fulfill over 90 percent of your cooking needs.

Do learn to use it to the full. I've written this Encyclopedia of Microwave Cooking to give you the maximum knowledge and use of your Microwave as I can.

Remember that a microwave oven will prove as fruitful as your experiments with it, so learn to use it to the full with your own recipes. To adapt them, cook traditional recipes about one-fourth the time you would normally. Take my word, once you learn the Microwave Method, you will find yourself in the fast and convenient world of state-of-the-art cooking, and you will not want to do without one.

In closing, may I point out that a microwave oven can pay for itself in a few years through savings in the electricity it consumes.

It is **cool cooking** all the way! Because of this, you will enjoy cooking the **Microwave way** even on the warmest summer days.

Introduction

Understanding Microwave Cooking

There are basic principles to how a microwave oven works regardless of the brand. These are both interesting and important to understand.

First, understand that **Microwaves** are "radio frequency" waves called microwaves because they are very short in length.

The next important point is to realize that when microwaves enter anything containing water molecules, these are activated and move about so rapidly that they hit and rub against the food molecules, that movement causing friction on the molecular level thus producing heat which does the cooking.

How does the "Convection" part of a microwave oven work?

Simply like any other classic type of oven.
Example: Preheat oven to 350°F. (180°C) 15 minutes.
　　　　 Bake 40 minutes at 350°F. (180°C).
Look for pad indicating the above and proceed to enter the required temperature and time just as for any type of electric oven.

Residual Cooking

All foods, regardless of the time they take to cook, have a **residual** cooking period, which is the cooking that takes place in the food even after it is removed from the heat source or the oven.

So, remember that the heavier and denser a portion of food, the more residual cooking it will have.

It is also important to remember that in microwave cooking there is a greater amount of residual heat that stays in the food than in the **conventional** method of cooking. This is explained by the fact that during microwave cooking the water molecules present in all foods gain momentum, and it takes time for that momentum to subside, so while it exists more heat continues to be produced.

For instance, when a roast is taken from the microwave oven, its internal temperature can climb as much as 15 degrees in a standing time of 15 to 20 minutes. **This is important to know,** as in that period vegetables or other foods to be served with the meal can be cooked.

Stirring is another important factor in microwave cooking, because the heat is produced faster in the outer surfaces and around the dish than in the middle, so stirring once distributes the heat evenly. Of course, this does not apply to cakes or roast chicken, etc.

Why do we often refer to Microwaving as "cool cooking"?

Microwave cooking is called **cool cooking** because the heat is produced in the food and not in the oven. A covered container does not get hotter than an uncovered one because the steam is trapped in the dish. So, food does not stick or burn in the container.

The Water Molecules

Make sure to have food in your microwave oven before operating it. If there are no water molecules, always present in all foods, to **absorb** the **microwaves,** the pressure builds up in the oven. These waves can reflect back to the magnetron tube, which is the heart of the microwave oven, and damage or destroy it.

If you have young children who may play with it, take the good habit of keeping a glass of water in the microwave, so that whatever they do when touching the key, the oven will be operational.

Remember that the microwave oven cannot work with the door open or even slightly ajar.

650-700 W	500-600 W	400-500 W
15 seconds	18 seconds	21 seconds
30 seconds	36 seconds	42 seconds
45 seconds	54 seconds	1 minute
1 minute	1 min 10 sec.	1 min 25 sec.
2 minutes	2 min 30 sec.	2 min 45 sec.
3 minutes	3 min 30 sec.	4 minutes
4 minutes	4 min 45 sec.	5 min 30 sec.
5 minutes	6 minutes	7 minutes
6 minutes	7 min 15 sec.	8 min 25 sec.
7 minutes	8 min 25 sec.	9 min 45 sec.
8 minutes	9 min 30 sec.	11 minutes
9 minutes	10 min 45 sec.	12 min 30 sec.
10 minutes	12 minutes	14 minutes
15 minutes	18 minutes	20 minutes
20 minutes	24 minutes	27 minutes
25 minutes	30 minutes	34 minutes
30 minutes	36 minutes	41 minutes

This chart gives you an idea of the time needed for any food you cook in an oven with the above wattage.

However, it is always wise, regardless of wattage, to check the cooking when 2 minutes of the cooking period still remain. That's assuming, of course, that the cooking time indicated is over 2 minutes.

Power Level Chart

Power	Output	Use
HIGH	100% .... (700 watts)	Boil water Brown ground meat Cook fresh fruits and vegetables Cook fish Cook poultry (up to 3 lb [1,5 kg]) Heat beverages (not containing milk) Make candy Preheat Browning Dish (accessory)
M. HIGH	90% .... (650 watts)	Heat frozen foods (not containing eggs or cheese) Heat canned foods Reheat leftovers Warm baby food
MEDIUM	70% .... (490 watts)	Bake cakes Cook meats Cook shellfish Prepare eggs and delicate food
M. LOW	50% .... (360 watts)	Bake muffins Cook custards Melt butter and chocolate Prepare rice
LOW	27% .... (200 watts)	Less tender cuts of meat Simmer stews and soups Soften butter and cheese
WARM	10% .... (70 watts)	Keep foods at serving temperature Rise yeast breads Soften ice cream
"Defrost"	35% .... (245 watts)	All thawing, see Defrosting Charts
"Delay Stand"	0% .... (0 watts)	Start heating at later time Program stand time after cooking

IMPI — International Microwave Power Institute — is an international institution governing microwave data throughout the world for kitchens, hospitals, etc.
IMPI have set the standards which have been adopted with regard to the designation of Power Settings for Microwave Ovens:
HIGH, MEDIUM-HIGH, MEDIUM, MEDIUM-LOW, LOW, REHEAT, DEFROST, START, which must be observed everywhere in the world.

Variable Power

This describes the choice of power levels that allow you to prepare food in the microwave which normally would be over sensitive to continuous microwave activity. To easily understand this process, it is actually an "on and off" cycle timed for varying amounts of microwave energy, which means that this pulsating action effectively creates slower cooking activity, without your having to worry about it. If your recipe calls for 1/2 power, this equals MEDIUM-LOW, which is like constant simmering. When microwave cooking first began, ovens had only "Cook" and "Defrost" cycles. Some of you may still have these ovens, so remember that you effectively "simmer" on the Defrost cycle or whenever 1/2 power or MEDIUM is called for. For all other cooking, use the Cook cycle and add a few minutes to the cooking period called for in the recipe.

There are many other ways to cook in the various microwave ovens, so always be ready to give serious attention to your oven manual, and you will soon find it is all very easy.

Time Factors

Does anything affect the microwave cooking time? Yes, there are four major influences:

1. **The starting temperature of the food** will influence the total cooking time.
   Example: The colder the food, the longer it must cook.
2. **The density of the food** also affects its cooking period. A lightweight, porous food will cook much faster than a dense, solid food.
   Example: A large roll will cook so much faster in relation to a potato. The roll is lightweight and very porous, so it will be piping hot in 1 minute or sometimes less, but a potato will take 3 to 4 times as long because of its density.
3. Another important factor is the **total amount of food cooking in the oven at a single time.**
   Example: 2 slices of bacon will cook in 1 minute, but 4 slices will take 1½ or 2 minutes. As there is no fast rule about how to increase the cooking period when increasing the amount of food, it is advisable to take note if you do increase the time by adding one quarter or half the time. One point that helps when you wish to know **how much time** is needed for a favorite sauce or vegetable, etc. is to take note of the **weight or quantity** of the food, also the type of container, and whether it was covered or uncovered. This may seem involved, but it is very easy to understand and to remember.
4. **The shape of the cooking container also affects the cooking time.**
   A large, shallow container will cook the same amount of food faster than a deeper container of the same capacity, simply because the more surface area of food is exposed to the microwaves, the more heat can be generated and the faster the food will cook.

How to arrange food in the microwave

It is important to remember that food cooks more quickly at the outer edge of the container. Also, it cooks more slowly in the center of the dish. Place the largest or densest or thickest part of any piece of food toward the outer edge of the plate. Place thinner or small pieces in the center. This way it will even out the irregularly shaped pieces of food. For instance, irregularly shaped potatoes are best placed spoke-fashion with the smaller end toward the middle and the large end out. Cover the food to be reheated with a piece of waxed paper.

What is "conduction" in the microwave oven

Heat is generated in the **outer** layers of the food by what is called **Conduction,** which is the slow way for heat to reach the center of a food we wish to cook. In sauces, vegetables, and many other foods, stirring generates the heat in the outer layers and will reach the center of the food by conduction, which is the slow way for heat to travel through food and is helped by stirring cold food from the center of the food mass, which in turn is heated while the food that had been warmed up is taken to the center.

Standing time

This is one of the most important points to remember in microwave cooking.
It is the time needed in many foods between the point at which they are taken from the microwave oven to the point at which they are served. This is an important moment, which is needed to allow residual cooking to take place.
The heavier and denser a food, the more standing time is needed.
Example: a cake needs less standing time than a pie.

Degree of Moisture in Food

(1) The degree of moisture in food:
   the higher it is: faster and shorter cooking period;
   the lower it is: slower and longer cooking period.
(2) The quantity of liquid added to the food:
   the greater the quantity, the longer the cooking period will be.
(3) The density of produce:
   Porous = faster cooking: tomatoes, spinach, mushrooms, etc.
   More dense = longer cooking: peas, cauliflower, etc.
(4) Room temperature is the ideal temperature to start cooking:
   Fresh picked from the garden or at room temperature: faster cooking.
   Colder temperature: food taken from refrigerator or after thawing: longer cooking.
(5) The structure of the food:
   Smaller pieces = faster cooking: a small potato.
   Larger pieces = longer cooking: a large potato.
(6) Certain foods are covered during the cooking period, as indicated in the recipe, to prevent the natural moisture from evaporating.
(7) The degree of sugar content determines the degree of heat produced:
   The more sugar, the more intense the heat and the shorter the cooking period: syrup, caramel, etc.
(8) The more fat in food, the faster it will cook.
(9) The arrangement of the food plays an important role:
   4 to 5 potatoes placed in a circle will cook faster than if they were simply placed in the oven.

   Degree of moisture - adding of water - density - thickness - structure - covers - amount of sugar - degree of fat - arrangement of food - appropriate accessories - are all key words relating your cooking to the factors of heat, weight and temperature.

How food is cooked in the Microwave Oven

Microwaves are a form of high frequency radio wave similar to those used by a radio including AM, FM, and CB.
Electricity is converted into microwave energy by the magnetron tube, and microwaves are approximately four to six inches (10 to 15 cm) long with a diameter of about one-fourth inch (6 mm). From the magnetron tube, microwave energy is transmitted to the oven cavity where it is: reflected, transmitted and absorbed.

Reflection
Microwaves are reflected by metal just as a ball is bounced off a wall. That is why the inside of the oven is metal covered with epoxy. A combination of stationary (interior walls) and rotating metal (turntable or stirrer fan) helps assure that the microwaves are well distributed within the oven cavity to produce even cooking.

Transmission

Microwaves pass through some materials such as paper, glass and plastic much like sunlight shining through a window. Because these substances do not absorb or reflect the microwave energy, they are ideal materials for microwave oven cooking containers.

Absorption

During heating, microwaves will be absorbed by food. They penetrate to a depth of about 3/4 to 1½ inches (2 to 4 cm). Microwave energy excites the molecules in the food (especially water, fat and sugar molecules), and causes them to vibrate at a rate of 2,450,000,000 times per second. This vibration causes friction, and heat is produced. If you vigorously rub your hands together, you will feel heat produced by friction. The internal cooking is then done by conduction. **The heat** which is produced by friction is conducted to the center of the food.

Foods also continue to cook by conduction during standing time, which keeps the cooked food warm for 4 to 10 minutes after cooking, and makes it possible to cook 3 to 4 dishes with only one oven, and to serve everything warm.

How to cook a complete meal in the Microwave Oven

If your menu calls for a roast, potatotes and green peas, cook the roast first. During its waiting period, cook the potatoes, they will remain warm from 20 to 30 minutes covered with a cloth, then the vegetable with the shortest cooking period.

The dessert may be cooked before the meat, or if it is to be served hot, cook it during the meal and let it stand in the oven. The oven goes off when the bell rings, and the food may be left inside until it is time to serve it.

Magnetic Turntable

Some ovens are equipped with an automatic magnetic turntable or a small fan in the top of the oven, or an invisible rotating system (whichever is featured in your Microwave, will be explained in your instruction manual), then you do not have to rotate the dish.

If your Microwave has neither turntable, nor fan, nor invisible rotating system, then you will have to rotate the dish for even cooking as the Microwave may tend to focus more on a definite spot in the food, especially if there is fat in the meat, and remember that they are not always visible. What happens is that the fat parts cook more quickly because the reflection area is not altered, so, of course the cooking dish may be rotated.

A few questions often asked

"Can I cook two or three foods together in my microwave oven?"

It can be done, but I am personally against it, as it is more difficult to judge the cooking time of each one, and this could become rather involved. What is important to know is how long a food should be cooked and how long it will remain hot. For example, a potato takes 2 to 4 minutes at HIGH depending on its size, but 4 to 6 potatoes will take 8 to 12 minutes at HIGH depending on their size. Being dense they will remain very hot for 6 to 10 minutes, as long as they are covered with a paper or a cover.

"Can I season my food?"

Yes, by all means, microwaved food has only one enemy, **salt.** It should be added after or in the last 2 minutes of cooking because salt has an osmotic effect on foods, which means that it takes the water out of the food and tends to toughen it. So add salt to taste when the food is cooked.

"Can I brown steaks, sausages, hamburgers, etc., in my microwave oven?"
If your oven does not have a broiling unit, use the **Browning Dish** (with the brand name of Corning). It comes in different sizes, some even have a cover to keep the food hot. The **Browning Dish,** regardless of size and shape, works by the same principle. Like all super inventions it is simple. Each one has a **special thin oxide base undercoating.** When the empty dish is preheated in the microwave oven for 3 to 7 minutes at HIGH, the time depending on the recipe, what happens is that the special coating interacts with microwave energy and produces heat. As the browning dish has little feet which raise it above the microwave oven shelf, the shelf cannot steal heat from the dish and break it. Another asset is that there is no need to brown any kind of fat in the dish. Once it is heated, place in it the prepared meat, without taking the dish from the oven. With your finger tips press down the meat to obtain a perfect contact between the dish and the meat. Cook according to the time required by the recipe. Turn the meat, such as chops or steaks, etc.; they will have an appetizing brown color. Let stand in the hot dish, without additional cooking but for the same length of time that was used to brown the bottom of the meat. This is a super delicious way to brown a steak or any type of chop or hamburgers; they will not brown on top, but will be well cooked.
I also use my **Browning Dish** to make a Chinese "Stir-Fry" dinner.

The Perfection of Reheating in the Microwave Oven

The reheated foods taste fresh cooked. Through the years, I have found out that leftovers never taste like leftovers.

How to reheat cooked food in the Microwave Oven

A single pie portion: Set the piece of pie on a plate, reheat at MEDIUM-HIGH, 1 to 1½ minutes, according to thickness of the filling. Let stand 1 minute.
Doughnuts: 1 doughnut — 15 seconds at MEDIUM-HIGH.
           2 doughnuts — 20 to 30 seconds at MEDIUM-HIGH.
           3 doughnuts — 1 minute or a little less.
Rolls: Wrap in a white kitchen paper
         2 rolls — 15 to 16 seconds at MEDIUM-HIGH
         4 rolls — 20 to 30 seconds at MEDIUM-HIGH
Beware of overheating any of these, including a square of baked cake which will be hot in 15 seconds, always at MEDIUM-HIGH.
For any cooked foods I wish to warm up, I use MEDIUM-HIGH. When I am not sure of the time, I start with 15 seconds and add slowly what is needed.
It is a very good rule to let warmed up food stand for 1/2 to 1 minute before serving.
To reheat a plate of meat and vegetables, cover food with waxed paper and reheat at MEDIUM-HIGH from 1 to 1½ minutes, depending on the quantity. Let stand 1 minute before serving.
Another exciting factor when reheating food in the microwave oven is that it tastes fresh-cooked.

Fresh Tomato Sauce (p. 77) →

16

Introduction to Metric Measures

Millilitre (mL): replaces the fluid ounce
Litre (L): replaces the quart
Gram (g): replaces the ounce
Kilogram (kg): replaces the pound
Degrees Celslum (°C): replaces
  degrees Fahrenheit
Centimetre (cm): replaces the inch

250 mL replaces an 8-ounce cup
15 mL replaces 1 tablespoon
5 mL replaces 1 teaspoon
1 kg a little more than 2 pounds
500 g a little more than 1 pound
100°C water boils
5 cm about 2 inches

Metric Equivalents of Most Used Measures in Cooking

Teaspoon:
1/4 teaspoon . . . . 1 mL
1/2 teaspoon . . . . 2 mL
1 teaspoon . . . . 5 mL
2 teaspoon . . . . 10 mL

Tablespoon:
1 tablespoon . . . . 15 mL
2 tablespoons . . . . 30 mL
3 tablespoons . . . . 50 mL
4 tablespoons . . . . 60 mL
2 to 3 tablespoons . . . . 30 to 50 mL
4 to 6 tablespoons . . . . 60 to 90 mL

Cups:
1/4 cup . . . . 60 mL
1/3 cup . . . . 80 mL
1/2 cup . . . . 125 mL
3/4 cup . . . . 190 mL
1 cup . . . . 250 mL
1¼ cups . . . . 315 mL
1⅓ cups . . . . 330 mL
1½ cups . . . . 375 mL
2 cups . . . . 500 mL
3 cups . . . . 750 mL
4 cups . . . . 1 L
5 cups . . . . 1.25 L
6 cups . . . . 1.5 L

Temperatures
150°F . . . . 65°C
200°F . . . . 95°C
250°F . . . . 120°C
300°F . . . . 150°C
350°F . . . . 180°C
400°F . . . . 200°C
425°F . . . . 225°C
450°F . . . . 230°C
500°F . . . . 260°C

← Top : Côte d'Azur Noodles (p. 47)
← Bottom : Delight of the Sea Macaroni Salad (p. 43)

Rice

Rice

Rice is the oldest and most cultivated grain in the world.

The Chinese date their first cultivation of rice back 5000 years. By the Fourth Century B.C. rice had reached Egypt by way of Persia, like so many of our foods and customs which we take for granted nowadays.

Then as the years passed, in 1686 a ship from Madagascar, landing in a South Carolina city for repairs, expressed gratitude by leaving a bag of rice, which the Fathers of the city quickly planted, as they had been told, in a swamp near their city, and to their amazement it yielded almost enough to feed the colony. And so, the USA had entered into rice production. Today, Texas, Arkansas, Louisiana and California are the major American rice producers.

As you may realize when reading these few lines, rice has through the centuries circled around the earth and has played an important, I would say, vital role in the history of humanity and will continue to do so in future, feeding millions of people.

Think of the famous "Rissoto Milanese" of Italy, which by the way cooks beautifully in the microwave oven, and was first made in the Po Valley, where they started to grow rice in the 15th century.

In Japan, rice planting is a time of happy celebration. In Osaka, on June 14th, a dozen country girls are chosen to perform the ceremony of transplanting seedlings in the rice paddy fields of Sumihochu Shrine. Ten years ago, I was happy to have the privilege to see this celebration.

Another interesting fact in Japan is that the word for rice is "Gohan" which is also used for **Meals**, since no meal is complete without a bowl of rice.

Varieties of Rice Available

Short Grain Rice
Why short grain? Because the shorter the grain the shorter the growing time, and the higher the yield the lower the cost.

Shorter grain rice is the most moist, it takes less water to cook it and the grains cling more to each other. The best of all types of rice for puddings, rice croquettes, rice rings, etc.

Long Grain Rice
Long Grain Rice is a rice 3 to 4 times longer, and whiter than the short grain type. Properly cooked, the grains separate from each other.

Long grain rice may be used whenever you wish to serve rice, but it is especially perfect for salads, or to serve mixed with vegetables or to replace potatoes. It is also more costly than short grain rice.

Parboiled Rice
A rice that is steamed or put through a hot water processing before being polished, which allows water soluble proteins to permeate the starch part of the rice and remain there. It has a light golden color and requires more cooking time. It is also the most costly of all rice. It can be used in the same manner as long grain rice.

Brown Rice
All kernels are unpolished which gives them their light brown color. It is important to know that brown rice retains much of its bran layers which contain its natural oil, proteins and vitamins.
It has a chewier consistency than polished or long grain rice and also has a nutty flavor, of which I am personally very fond, especially when served with roasted or broiled meats.
Because of all its qualities, it is somewhat longer to cook than polished rice.

Quick Cooking or Instant Rice
The best available is the **long grain** type. It is a pre-steamed long grain rice that only needs to be heated quickly in boiling water. It is ready to use or serve in just minutes.

Wild Rice
Not really rice at all, but the seed of a marsh grass. The grains are long, dark greenish in color, more chewy when cooked than other rice.
Wild rice is gathered by hand, which explains its high cost, it is also considered a gourmet delicacy, whichever way it is served. It is gathered from lakes in the deep green forests of Minnesota, Wisconsin and all the neighboring parts of Canada. In the spring, limp shoots of an aquatic grass appear in these lakes. By late fall they stand tall and produce an edible seed, the "Wild Rice", name given by the Indians who, as early as the First Century A.D., began to harvest, dry and thresh the seeds. It was the major source of carbohydrate in their diet.
We tend to forget that the commercialization of wild rice began in the early 1600's when the "Voyageurs", "Coureur de Bois" and fur traders began to follow the natural eating habits of the Indians living in the lake region, which was a diet of game and fish with wild rice and wild berries. Starting in the mid 1970's, 95% of the wild rice came to be produced in the now cultivated wild rice paddies of USA and Canada. But the important point to be aware of is that wild rice is low in calories and fat, yet high in fiber and good quality protein, it also has a variety of minerals and vitamins with no or very little preservatives.

The Advantages of Rice

As there are small modifications in the cooking of rice depending on the brand used, it is advisable to read the directions given on the package. What is also fascinating about rice is its faculty to be everything, apart from being nourishing. It can be used in soups, served as a vegetable, as a main course, as a dessert, as a baby food, etc., and does so for people all around the world.
An important, scarcely known fact is that rice has a wonderful and almost unique quality: it is able to absorb the impact of heavy food so you can even eat more without that too full feeling.
I hope you will enjoy the following rice recipes done so quickly and so easily with perfect results when cooked by the microwave method. You will also, I am sure, appreciate the versatility and outstanding nutritional value of rice.

Rice Cooking Chart

Item	Container	Amount of hot water	Approx. time to boil water at HIGH (in minutes)	Approx. time to cook rice at MEDIUM-LOW (in minutes)	Stand time (in minutes)
Long Grain (1 cup) (250 mL)	8-cup (2 L) casserole	2 cups (500 mL)	4 to 5	14 to 16	10
Short Grain (1 cup) (250 mL)	8-cup (2 L) casserole	2 cups (500 mL)	4 to 5	10 to 12	10
Quick Cooking (1 cup) (250 mL)	4-cup (1 L) casserole	1 cup (250 mL)	2 to 3	5	5
Brown Rice (1 cup) (250 mL)	8-cup (2 L) casserole	3 cups (750 mL)	5 to 6	45 to 50	15
Wild Rice* (1 cup) (250 mL)	8-cup (2 L) casserole	4 cups (1 L)	6	30 to 40	15

Depending on the type of wild rice, cooking time can vary from 25 minutes to 40 minutes. Stir once at half the cooking time. When cooking time is finished, let stand 10 minutes, stir with a fork, taste one grain, if you wish.
If you prefer to have a softer wild rice, add 1/2 cup (125 mL) hot water, stir with a fork. Microwave another 8 to 10 minutes at MEDIUM HIGH. Let stand 15 minutes. Stir with a fork and finish according to your recipe.

To Cook Rice Automatically

If your oven has the Automatic or Instamatic type of cooking, this is the way to proceed to cook your rice. The time is of little concern since the oven itself will determine that. Consult your oven Manual for instructions.

The quantity of rice and water remain the same as in the Rice Cooking Chart. It must be covered during the cooking period.

How to Cook Rice Starting in Cold Water

If you consider cooking rice a mystery, try this method. It will never fail you. You will realize how easy it is.

> **2 cups (500 mL) water, at room temperature**
> **1/2 tsp. (2 mL) salt**
> **1 tbsp. (15 mL) vegetable or olive oil**
> **1 cup (250 mL) short or long grain rice**

Put the water, salt and oil in an 8-cup (2 L) dish, with a cover. Stir in the rice. Microwave 10 minutes at HIGH. Stir well, cover, microwave 15 minutes at MEDIUM for short grain, 20 minutes at MEDIUM for long grain. Let stand covered, without stirring, 10 to 15 minutes.
If you add butter or herbs or cooked vegetables, add only after standing time and stir with a fork.

Interesting Variations
Use homemade or diluted canned consommé or tomato juice to replace the above water.
Add to the water 2 tablespoons (30 mL) dried soup vegetables or 1 tablespoon (15 mL) of a dried herb of your choice.
Replace water with chicken or beef broth, or tomato or apple juice to make curried rice.

How to Cook Wild Rice

The following method for cooking wild rice, referred to as **New Quick Soak Method,** was developed by food specialists at the Ontario Food Council.
I had adopted it as the best method I had ever used, since it is also the one that retains the best attributes of flavor and texture of wild rice.

> **1 cup (250 mL) wild rice**
> **3 cups (750 mL) water**
> **1 tsp. (5 mL) salt**

Place rice in a sieve and rinse under cold running water until the water runs clear.
Measure the water in a 6-cup (1.5 L) dish. Microwave 6 minutes at HIGH. Add the rice and salt. Stir well, cover and microwave 20 to 30 minutes at MEDIUM. Stir with a fork. Cover and let stand 25 minutes. Taste for doneness. If ever it needs more cooking, which can happen with wild rice, give it another 5 minutes at MEDIUM. Let stand 10 minutes. Serve.

Cooking Yield of Different Types of Rice

- 1 cup (250 mL) uncooked, **long, medium** or **short grain** rice yields about 3 cups (750 mL) when cooked.
- 1 cup (250 mL) uncooked **Converted** or **Parboiled** rice yields about 4 cups (1 L) when cooked.
- 1 cup (250 mL) **Instant** or **Quick Cooking** rice yields about 2 cups (500 mL) when cooked.
- 1 cup (250 mL) uncooked **Wild** rice yields from 3 to 4 cups (750 mL to 1 L), when cooked, according to type.

Varieties of Rice →

Interesting variations on plain boiled rice

(Any type of rice can be used)
1. For a golden colored rice, add 1/4 teaspoon (60 mL) of turmeric to the water before adding the rice. Excellent and colorful with fish and egg dishes.
2. To 3 cups (750 mL) of cooked rice, add 2 tablespoons (30 mL) fresh lemon juice, 1 teaspoon (5 mL) grated lemon rind and salt to taste. Serve with chicken, veal or meat loaf.
3. Toss cooked rice with butter to taste, add chives or parsley, 4 to 5 slices of diced microwaved bacon, and 1 tablespoon (15 mL) sour cream. Serve with roast chicken or veal or pork.
4. Vegetarian Rice, to serve as is or with veal roast or boiled chicken. To 3 cups (750 mL) cooked rice,* add 1 cup (250 mL) thinly sliced raw mushrooms, 1/4 cup (60 mL) sliced black olives, an equal amount of slivered almonds, 1/2 cup (125 mL) grated cheese of your choice, 1/4 teaspoon (1 mL) salt and pepper to taste. Serve as is or shape into a ring by simply buttering a ring mold and packing the cheese mixture into it.
   If the shaped rice is cold and you would prefer to have it hot, cover with waxed paper when ready to serve, microwave 4 minutes at MEDIUM, in its mold. Unmold on serving dish. Fill to your taste.

   * 1 cup (250 mL) uncooked rice will give you 3 cups (750 mL) cooked rice.

To Reheat Cooked Rice

Place cold cooked rice in a dish. Drizzle on top 1 tablespoon (15 mL) cold water for each cup of cooked rice. Do not stir. Cover dish and warm up at MEDIUM 6 to 8 minutes. Stir with a fork, test rice. If not hot enough give it another minute or 2.

Method 2 to Reheat Rice
Place the cooked rice in a plastic sieve. Place over a dish of hot water. Top with waxed paper, warm up at MEDIUM 2 to 3 minutes, depending on the quantity of rice. Stir with a fork.

How to Freeze Rice

Rice freezes well, but takes as long to thaw and reheat as to cook from raw.
But this is important knowledge if at any time you have leftover cooked rice to use as needed.
- Plain cooked rice placed in a well-covered dish will keep for 5 to 6 months in the freezer.
- To use, thaw one to two hours at room temperature.
- Another way to thaw cooked rice is to place 1 or 2 cups (250 to 500 mL) in a plate at room temperature for 20 minutes, then in the microwave oven for 10 minutes at LOW. Stir with a fork and repeat operation, if necessary, while checking the rice after 5 minutes.

← Top : Minty Rice (p. 29)
← Bottom : Risi Pisi (p. 27)

25

Coconut Water

Excellent to cook rice in when to be used for curried rice or dessert.
Combine in a bowl 1 cup (250 mL) milk, 1 cup (250 mL) water and 1 cup (250 mL) grated unsweetened coconut*. Microwave at MEDIUM 3 minutes. Let cool, then strain through a fine sieve, pressing hard on the coconut. Use as part of the liquid demanded by the recipe.
Yield: 1 cup (250 mL).

You may buy a fresh coconut and grate it. Use the coconut milk as part of the milk required in the recipe.

Akni Rice Water

India gave us this super recipe for cooking rice. The Akni water in which the rice is cooked gives it a delicate, exciting flavor.

1 onion cut in half, thinly sliced

2 - 3 garlic cloves, crushed

A 2-inch (5 cm) piece of fresh ginger root

1 tbsp. (15 mL) fennel seeds

1 tbsp. (15 mL) coriander seeds

1/2 tsp. (2 mL) cardamom seeds

4 cups (1 L) water

Akni Rice Pilaff

1 - 2 tbsp. (15 - 30 mL) butter

1 medium-sized onion, thinly sliced

1/2 tsp. (2 mL) cardamom

4 whole cloves

1 or 2-inch (2.5 - 5 cm) cinnamon stick

2 cups (500 mL) long grain rice

Prepare Akni Water:

Place in a bowl the sliced onion, the garlic and fresh ginger. Then, tie loosely in a piece of cotton or cheesecloth, the fennel, coriander and cardamom seeds and add to the onion mixture. Pour the water on top and microwave 5 minutes at HIGH. Cool and remove spice bag when ready to use.

To Make the Pilaff:

Melt the butter in a 4-cup (1 L) dish 1 minute at HIGH, add the onion, whole cloves, cardamom and cinnamon stick. Stir in the uncooked rice until the grains are coated with the butter, add the 4 cups (1 L) of Akni Water, cover and microwave 15 minutes at MEDIUM-HIGH, stirring after 5 minutes of cooking. According to the type of rice used, the cooking period could vary, so check the rice. When it is cooked, add a piece of butter to taste and serve.
This Akni Rice Pilaff freezes very well, so it is advisable to prepare the 2 cups (500 mL) of rice, which will give you 6 cups (1.5 L) when cooked. Use what you require and freeze the rest in a microwave-safe dish. To thaw out, simply place the dish with the frozen rice in the microwave for 4 to 6 minutes at HIGH, stirring once. As the rice is already cooked, be careful not to overcook it when reheating.

Sweet Rice

A super breakfast cereal, with little work and short cooking period; prepare the day before and simply reheat in your plate, 1 to 3 minutes at MEDIUM. As a dessert, serve at room temperature topped with cream and maple syrup. As a variation, sprinkle top with chopped nuts of your choice or peeled and diced fresh fruit, such as peaches, pears, apples, oranges or pitted cherries, the quantity is according to taste.

1/2 cup (125 mL) short grain rice	4 tbsp. (60 mL) sugar or brown or maple sugar
1½ cups (375 mL) milk	1/4 tsp. (1 mL) nutmeg or cinnamon or
3 tbsp. (50 mL) butter	the grated rind of 1 orange

Put the rice and the milk in a 4-cup (1 L) bowl, cover and microwave at MEDIUM 20 minutes. Add the butter, sugar or brown or maple sugar, the spice of your choice or the orange rind. Stir well with a fork. Cover and microwave 5 to 8 minutes at MEDIUM. Stir with a fork, when ready to serve. Equally good hot or cold.
To reheat, add a spoonful or two of milk or cream simply poured on top of the rice. Do not stir, cover and microwave at MEDIUM 2 to 3 minutes according to quantity.

Risi Pisi *(photo opposite page 25 bottom)*

An Italian speciality which comes from Venice. I always make one to serve with chicken livers, or with the first green peas on the market or in the garden, usually at the end of June. Serve as is with chicken, sausages or liver.

3 slices bacon, diced	2 cups (500 mL) fresh green peas*
4 green onions, peeled and diced	1/4 cup (60 mL) minced fresh parsley
2 tbsp. (30 mL) butter	3 cups (750 mL) hot water or
1 tbsp. (15 mL) vegetable oil	chicken consommé
1 cup (250 mL) long grain rice	

Place the bacon in an 8-cup (2 L) microwave-safe dish. Microwave 1 minute at HIGH. Add the green onions and the butter. Microwave 2 minutes at MEDIUM-HIGH. Stir well. Add the vegetable oil and the rice. Stir until the whole is well mixed, add the green peas, stir again. Add the parsley and hot water or chicken consommé. Stir again. Cover and cook 20 minutes at MEDIUM. Stir with a fork, test the doneness of the green peas and the rice. If necessary, microwave another 5 minutes at MEDIUM. Let stand 5 minutes and serve.

* *When fresh green peas are not available, replace by an equal quantity of unthawed frozen green peas. Do not change the cooking period.*

Turkish Pilaff

Turkish Pilaff is perfect to serve with roast lamb or pork and all types of chicken dishes. A pilaff is a dish with rice, first rolled in butter melted in the microwave, then flavored and cooked.

1/4 cup (60 mL) butter or vegetable oil

1 medium-sized onion, chopped fine

1 cup (250 mL) long grain rice

1/4 tsp. (1 mL) cinnamon

A pinch of allspice or cloves

2 cups (500 mL) hot chicken consommé

1 tsp. (5 mL) salt, pepper to taste

1/4 cup each (60 mL) currants and chopped nuts

Melt the butter or heat the oil 2 minutes at HIGH in a 6-cup (1.5 L) dish. Add the onion, stir well, microwave 2 minutes at HIGH. Add the rice. Stir until well coated with the onion butter. Microwave 3 minutes at HIGH, stirring after 2 minutes of cooking. Add all the remaining ingredients, except the chopped nuts. Microwave 20 minutes at MEDIUM-LOW. Add the chopped nuts. Stir the whole with a fork. Serve.

Dried Fruit Pilaff *(photo opposite page 41 top)*

If you roast a large chicken or barbecue meats of your choice in the summer, try this Indian Dried Fruit Pilaff to serve with it.

3 tbsp. (50 mL) butter

1 cup (250 mL) long grain or parboiled rice

2 cups (500 mL) hot water

1/2 tsp. (2 mL) salt

2 tbsp. (30 mL) butter

1/3 cup (80 mL) dried apricots, slivered

1/3 cup (80 mL) dried prunes, quartered

1/4 cup (60 mL) dried currants

1 tbsp. (15 mL) honey

2 tbsp. (30 mL) hot water

Melt the butter 2 minutes at HIGH in an 8-cup (2 L) microwave-safe dish. Stir in the rice, until well buttered. Add the hot water and salt. Cover, microwave 20 minutes at MEDIUM. Let stand.
In another dish, melt the remaining butter, add the slivered apricots, the quartered dried prunes and the currants. Stir well, add the honey and hot water. Microwave at MEDIUM-LOW 5 minutes, covered. Stir and pour over the hot rice.
Serve with the meat or as a dessert with a dish of yogurt used as a topping.

Minty Rice *(photo opposite page 25 top)*

A friend of mine, very involved in vegetarian health food cuisine, serves this dish as a light luncheon dish, with a bowl of crunchy watercress. I serve it hot with cold or hot thinly sliced chicken, or as a garnish for sliced cooked ham.

3 tbsp. (50 mL) butter or margarine	1/4 cup (60 mL) chopped fresh mint leaves
1 onion, peeled and thinly sliced	1/4 cup (60 mL) chopped parsley leaves
1 cup (250 mL) brown rice	3/4 cup (190 mL) natural yogurt
2½ cups (625 mL) chicken consommé	Salt, pepper to taste

Melt the butter 1 minute at HIGH in an 8-cup (2 L) dish. Add the onion, stir until well coated with the butter. Microwave 2 minutes at HIGH. Stir and add the brown rice, chicken consommé, mint and parsley leaves. Cover and microwave 45 to 50 minutes at MEDIUM-LOW.
When cooked, add the yogurt, salt and pepper to taste. Stir with a fork. Serve.

Rice and Cheese Casserole
Convection

Quick and simple to prepare, it can be served as a main dish with a green salad or as a casserole with hard cooked eggs in white sauce, or cold thinly sliced meat.

1 cup (250 mL) short grain rice	1/4 cup (60 mL) chopped parsley
2 cups (500 mL) grated Cheddar cheese	4 green onions, chopped fine
1/2 cup (125 mL) milk	1 cup (250 mL) coarse breadcrumbs
1/2 cup (125 mL) light cream	3 tbsp. (50 mL) melted butter

Microwave the rice according to directions in the **Rice Cooking Chart** (see Index). Butter an 8 x 8-inch (20 x 20 cm) microwave-safe dish. Make alternate layers of rice and cheese until all is used.
Mix the milk and cream with the parsley and green onions. Pour over the rice and cheese.
Stir the breadcrumbs with the melted butter. Spread over the rice and cheese. Bake by the Convection Method of your Microwave oven at 350°F. (180°C) about 30 minutes or until light brown on top.
Serve hot.

Cheese Rice Ring *(photo opposite page 73 top)*

What an elegant way to serve a creamed leftover meat, chicken or fish, or filled with cooked fresh garden vegetables in the summer, or simply topped with a cheese sauce to serve as is.

2 cups (500 mL) uncooked short grain rice
1/2 cup (125 mL) grated cheese of your choice

1/4 cup (60 mL) melted butter
Salt to taste

Microwave the rice according to the **Rice Cooking Chart** (see Index). To the hot rice, add the grated cheese, melted butter and salt. Stir with a fork until the whole is well blended.
Butter a ring mold, fill with the rice, bringing it well up to the top of the mold. This is important because when the mold is not properly filled it can break when turned out.
Place mold in a pan when ready to unmold, add hot water to the pan holding the mold. Microwave 5 minutes at MEDIUM to warm up the rice. Loosen rice around the edges and unmold by inverting **quickly** on a hot platter. Fill as you choose. Serve.

Molded Rice

An easy way to make a rice ring of various forms, depending on the dish being used. It can be filled with creamed chicken or steamed seafood or cooked vegetables, or as a dessert, filled with poached fruit or a chocolate or lemon or orange cream.

2 cups (500 mL) cold water
1/2 tsp. (2 mL) salt
2 tsp. (10 mL) butter or margarine
1 cup (250 mL) short grain rice

1/4 tsp. (1 mL) grated nutmeg or
the grated rind of 1 lemon
1/4 cup (60 mL) butter

Place the cold water, 1/2 teaspoon (2 mL) salt and the 2 teaspoons (10 mL) butter or margarine in an 8-cup (2 L) bowl. Microwave 10 minutes at HIGH. Add the rice and the grated nutmeg or the grated lemon rind. Microwave 10 to 12 minutes at MEDIUM-LOW, covered. Stir gently with a fork, the water should be all absorbed and the grains soft. Cover, let stand 15 minutes. Butter the mold of your choice, a ring mold or a round mold. Press the cooked rice in it. Melt the remaining butter 2 minutes at HIGH. Pour over the molded rice. Cover with a plate or a square of waxed paper. Microwave 8 to 9 minutes at MEDIUM. Let stand 5 minutes.
Loosen the edges and turn out onto a platter. Fill center as you please.
Variation: Add a spoonful or two of diced pimento or minced chives or fresh tarragon to taste, or 1/2 or 3/4 cup (125 to 190 mL) of cooked frozen green peas.

Summer Rice Salad *(photo opposite page 32)*

For me this salad is a summer long pleasure, as it seems to be the perfect companion to all our summer foods. Super with cold boiled salmon.

1 cup (250 mL) uncooked long grain rice*	**Dressing:**
2 raw carrots, peeled and grated	1/2 tsp. (2 mL) salt
4 to 6 green onions, thinly sliced	1/4 tsp. (1 mL) pepper and dry mustard
1/4 cup (60 mL) chopped parsley	A good pinch of sugar
1/2 cup (125 mL) diced celery and leaves**	2 tbsp. (30 mL) cider or wine vinegar
1 cup (250 mL) cooked green peas	4 tbsp. (60 mL) oil of your choice

Microwave rice according to basic instructions for long grain rice in the **Rice Cooking Chart.** Cool and add the grated raw carrots, green onions, parsley, celery and leaves, and the cooked and cooled green peas.

Blend together the ingredients for the dressing. Pour over the rice mixture, toss lightly with a fork. Place in a bowl. To taste, top with a good spoonful of capers or 2 tablespoons (30 mL) of chopped nasturtium seeds (from the flowers***), or top the salad with nasturtium flowers which are edible and have a very nice peppery flavor, or with a good handful of minced lovage, or a handful of chopped walnuts. Any of the above are very nice on this salad; it is a matter of choice or availability. This recipe will yield 4 cups (1 L) of salad.

   * *Short grain rice can replace the long grain rice. Cook according to Rice Cooking Chart.*
  ** *When there are leaves on the celery stalks, use them.*
*** *Nasturtium seeds appear when the bloom falls. They may be kept in vinegar like pickles.*

Kedgeree

When the English were in India this **Kedgeree** became one of their favorite dishes. The best were made with long grain rice, in the Indian cuisine they preferred short grain rice. You will have to decide. This recipe was given to me by an English Canadian friend who made the best Kedgeree I ever tasted.

1 cup (250 mL) long grain rice	1 cup (250 mL) water
6 hard boiled eggs	1/2 to 1 lb (250 to 500 g) smoked salmon
1 cup (250 mL) milk	4 tbsp. (60 mL) butter

Microwave rice according to basic instructions in the Rice Cooking Chart*. Hard boil the eggs. Heat together the milk and water 4 minutes at HIGH pour over the smoked fish, cover and let stand 15 minutes. Drain fish in colander 15 minutes. Break up in pieces and add to the rice. Chop the hard boiled eggs into small pieces and add to the rice and fish.

Place the butter in a small dish and microwave 2 minutes at HIGH, pour into the rice mixture and stir with two forks to blend the whole. Add pepper to taste. This should be prepared the day before. Refrigerate overnight. To serve, lightly butter a microwave-safe dish. Pour in the rice and fish mixture. Cover with waxed paper. Microwave at MEDIUM 8 minutes, stir lightly with a fork, taste for seasoning. If the rice is not hot enough, add 2 minutes at a time at MEDIUM.

* *1 tablespoon (15 mL) of commercial chicken bouillon powder and 2 tablespoon (30 mL) of butter may be added to the rice before cooking.*

Brown Rice Salad *(photo opposite page 65 top)*

Totally different from the Summer Rice Salad, perfect with meat or barbecued hamburgers or shish-kebabs.

1 cup (250 mL) uncooked brown rice

2 tbsp. (30 mL) oil of your choice

1 small onion, peeled and thinly sliced

1 medium green pepper, cut into thin strips

1 small red pepper, cut into thin strips

1 tbsp. (15 mL) red wine vinegar or tarragon vinegar

Salt, pepper to taste

1/4 tsp. (1 mL) marjoram or basil

Microwave the brown rice according to directions for brown rice in the **Rice Cooking Chart** (see Index). In a 4-cup (1 L) microwave-safe dish, heat the oil 2 minutes at HIGH, add the onion, green and red peppers. Stir until well coated with the oil, microwave 4 minutes at MEDIUM-HIGH. Stir well and add the cooked brown rice and the remaining ingredients. Stir again, always with a fork. Microwave 2 minutes at MEDIUM. Stir with a fork, taste for seasoning. Serve hot or at room temperature, but not refrigerated as the rice would taste hard cooked.

Wild Rice Vegetable Casserole *(photo opposite page 73 bottom)*

Super to serve as a luncheon casserole. All that is needed to finish the meal is an interesting fruit dessert.

1 cup (250 mL) wild rice

3 cups (750 mL) water

1 tsp. (5 mL) salt

1/4 cup (60 mL) butter

1 large onion, chopped fine

1/2 lb (250 g) thinly sliced mushrooms

1 cup (250 mL) carrots, peeled and shredded

1/4 tsp. (1 mL) pepper

1 tsp. (5 mL) salt

1/2 cup (125 mL) light cream

1 egg lightly beaten

2 tbsp. (30 mL) brandy

1/4 cup (60 mL) minced parsley

Wash the wild rice thoroughly. Place the water in an 8-cup (2 L) pan. Add the salt. Microwave at HIGH 5 minutes. Add the wild rice. Microwave 20 minutes at MEDIUM.
Melt the butter 2 minutes at HIGH, add the chopped onion. Stir and microwave at HIGH 2 minutes. Add the mushrooms, microwave 2 minutes at HIGH, stir. Add onion and mushrooms to the cooked wild rice, stir well with a fork, add the shredded carrots, salt and pepper.
Mix together the remaining ingredients, stir into the cooked wild rice. Cover and microwave 20 minutes at MEDIUM. Taste for seasoning and serve.

Summer Rice Salad (p. 31) →

Chinese Fried Rice

A quick lunch, easy to make with leftover cooked rice or thawed out frozen cooked rice and leftover cooked meat.

4 tbsp. (60 mL) vegetable oil or bacon fat

1 cup (250 mL) cooked rice

4 chopped green onions

1/2 tsp. (2 mL) salt

1/2 to 1 cup (125 to 250 mL) thinly sliced cooked pork, veal or beef

1 or 2 eggs

2 tbsp. (30 mL) soy sauce

I like to use a **Browning Dish** to make this dish in the microwave oven. Preheat the empty Browning Dish 6 minutes at HIGH. Add the oil or bacon fat, heat 2 minutes at HIGH. Add the rice, stir until well coated with the oil. Add the green onions, salt, and meat of your choice. Stir well. Make a hole in the center, break 1 or 2 eggs into the hole. Microwave at MEDIUM 1 or 2 minutes*, then stir them into the rice and meat. Add the soy sauce, stir again. Microwave 2 minutes at MEDIUM. Stir and serve.

Microwave 1 minute for one egg and 2 minutes for 2 eggs.

Confetti Rice

This recipe is full of color and flavor. Any combination of vegetables to your taste can be used, or leftovers. Perfect with pork, veal or lamb. Another advantage is that it can be prepared hours ahead of time and reheated when ready to use.

2 cups (500 mL) boiling water

1 tsp. (5 mL) salt

1 cup (250 mL) long grain rice

2 carrots, peeled and shredded

1/2 cup (125 mL) finely diced celery

4 green onions, chopped fine

1 cup (250 mL) or 1/2 box frozen green peas or 1/4 cup (60 mL) diced green pepper

1 tbsp. (15 mL) butter or margarine

Fresh parsley, chives or dill to taste

Place all the ingredients in an 8-cup (2 L) baking dish. Stir well. Microwave, covered, 10 minutes at HIGH, stirring once. Check doneness and microwave one or two minutes more, if necessary. Let stand 10 minutes. Stir, taste for seasoning.

← Top : Baked Eggs and Cheese (p. 60)
← Bottom : Scandinavian Omelet (p. 62)

My Four-Bowl Rice Cream

Whenever I serve this dessert for a buffet, everyone comments on it and is intrigued with the "4" bowls of garnishes, for each one to use one or all, or any combination.

1/4 cup (60 mL) short grain rice	1 tsp. (5 mL) vanilla
2 cups (500 mL) light cream	2 egg whites
2 egg yolks	2 tbsp. (30 mL) sugar
4 tbsp. (60 mL) sugar	

Short grain rice will give a creamier pudding, the long grain will give a light pudding.
Place the rice and cream in a large bowl. Microwave at MEDIUM-HIGH 10 minutes, stirring once.
Beat the egg yolks with the 4 tablespoons (60 mL) sugar and the vanilla, until light and foamy. Add to the cooked rice, stir till thoroughly mixed. Microwave 2 minutes at MEDIUM. Stir well.
MEDIUM 1 minute. Pour into an elegant serving dish and around it place four attractive bowls filled as follows:

Bowl I
Thinly sliced canned peaches, drained and flavored with a few spoonfuls of sherry or brandy.

Bowl II
Toasted slivered almonds, prepared as follows in the microwave: 1/2 cup (125 mL) (or more, to your taste) of slivered almonds placed in a bowl with 2 tablespoons (30 mL) of butter, microwaved 1 to 2 minute at HIGH. Stir well, they should be golden color.

Bowl III
Shredded Coconut, sprinkled with a bit of nutmeg.

Bowl IV
Strawberry or raspberry jam.

My Own Wild Rice Chasseur

Mother made this casserole using brown rice, to serve with roast wild duck or deer steak. I use wild rice with roast duck or beef or pork. If you prefer, it can be made with half wild rice, half brown rice, following the same directions.

1½ cups (375 mL) cooked wild rice*	4 tbsp. (60 mL) chutney of your choice
2 tbsp. (30 mL) brandy	1/4 cup (60 mL) butter
1 tsp. (5 mL) curry powder	Salt and pepper to taste

Microwave 3/4 cup (190 mL) wild rice or half wild rice and half brown rice according to instructions for wild rice in the **Rice Cooking Chart.**
Place in a dish the brandy, curry powder and chutney. Microwave 1 minute at MEDIUM. Add to the cooked wild rice. Stir well with a fork. Add the butter, salt and pepper to taste. Stir, cover and microwave 4 minutes at MEDIUM, when ready to serve.

* Or half wild rice and half brown rice.

Wild Rice "à la Ferguson"
Convection

About 25 years ago, one of my departed friends gave me this wild rice casserole recipe, the best I have ever experienced. I consider it a great gift since I am able to pass it on to many others. One day I tested it in the microwave oven, it was even better. May it be your turn to enjoy it.

1 cup (250 mL) wild rice	1/4 tsp. (1 mL) thyme
3 tbsp. (50 mL) butter	3 medium carrots, grated
1 medium-sized onion, chopped fine	1½ cups (375 mL) chicken consommé
2 celery stalks, diced	1½ cups (375 mL) grated Cheddar cheese
1/2 cup (125 mL) chopped parsley	2 tbsp. (30 mL) butter, diced

Wash the wild rice under cold running water. Spread on a towel, let dry for 2 hours.
Place butter in a 6-cup (1.5 L) dish. Melt 2 minutes at HIGH. Add the onion, stir well, microwave 3 minutes at HIGH, stirring once after 2 minutes. Add the celery, parsley, thyme, carrots. Stir until well mixed.
Butter an 8 x 8-inch (20 x 20 cm) dish or a 6-cup (1.5 L) dish, fill with alternate layers of the cooked wild rice, vegetable mixture and grated cheese. Pour the chicken consommé over all. Cover, with the cover of the dish or a piece of foil paper.
Preheat the Convection part of your microwave to 350°F. (180°C), 10 minutes. Set the casserole on the oven rack and bake 1 hour. Serve.

Note: If you need your oven for other dishes to be cooked for the meal, bake the wild rice casserole first. When ready, keep covered, set on a wooden board, it will remain hot 35 to 45 minutes. Or bake and keep on kitchen counter for an hour or two, as needed. and warm up by microwave 8 minutes at MEDIUM HIGH, when ready to serve, replacing the foil wrap, if used to cover, with plastic wrap.

Bacon and Green Pepper Rice

An interesting flavored rice casserole, to serve as a light meal or to accompany a roast of pork or veal.

4 to 6 slices of bacon

3 tbsp. (50 mL) bacon drippings*

1 medium-sized onion, chopped fine

1 medium-sized green pepper, diced

1 19-oz (540 mL) can tomatoes

1/2 tsp. (2 mL) sugar

1/2 tsp. (2 mL) thyme or savory

1/2 cup (125 mL) long grain rice

1/2 cup (125 mL) grated Cheddar cheese

Place slices of bacon in a dish. Microwave at HIGH 2 to 3 minutes. Place cooked bacon on paper towelling.
To the fat remaining in the dish, add the onion and green pepper. Microwave 3 minutes at HIGH. Stir well. Add the tomatoes, sugar, thyme or savory. Stir, add the rice. Stir, microwave at MEDIUM 20 minutes, stirring after 15 minutes and testing the doneness of the rice. When rice is tender, sprinkle top of casserole with the grated cheese. Microwave 1 minute at HIGH. Serve.

Bacon drippings may be replaced by butter or any other fat.

Broccoli and Rice Casserole

This recipe was especially developed to use quick cooking rice. Any other vegetable of your choice may replace the broccoli.

2 cups (500 mL) hot water

1 envelope onion soup mix

2 cups (500 mL) quick cooking rice

2 tbsp. (30 mL) butter or margarine

1 tsp. (5 mL) salt

1/2 tsp. (2 mL) pepper

Juice and grated rind of one lemon

1 lb (500 g) fresh broccoli

Mix together the hot water and soup mix. Add the rice, butter or margarine, salt and pepper. Stir together and add the lemon juice and grated rind. Cover. Microwave 2 minutes at HIGH. Let stand 5 minutes.
Wash the broccoli, break up into flowerets and place in a microwave-safe dish with 1/2 cup (125 mL) water. Cover and microwave 5 minutes at HIGH. Drain and place in a baking dish, pour the rice mixture on top, sprinkle with grated cheese to taste. Microwave 2 minutes at HIGH.

Pasta

Pasta

Italy and **Pasta** seem to be synonymous, since for centuries the Italians have been growing the right type of semolina flour needed to make pasta.

The Chinese had made them for centuries before they were known to the Italians. Marco Polo was the one who brought them back from his first trip to Egypt, he had various types. An amusing Pasta fact from Northern China is the importance for them to prepare very long noodles; their length being a sign of longevity. They also make noodles from shrimp, rice, peas, corn and ming beans. It is also interesting to know that ravioli were eaten in Rome as early as in 1284.

The Japanese are also enthusiastic noodlers, also creating their own from wheat, rice and buckwheat. The Japanese noodles fall into two categories: (a) The **Udon** noodles, (b) the **Sôneb** (wheat flour noodles) and the **Soda** eaten cold in the summer and so delicious. Japanese noodles are delicate with a gentle flavor. They are excellent if you are on a diet as they are low in calories.

They also have **Green Tea Leaf** noodles and **Green Spinach** noodles, their unusual texture and taste are well worth the effort to look for them.

How to buy pasta

You have quite a choice. Basically they are all made in the same manner. However difficult it is to explain, each type of pasta is different and permits many variations. Also, be aware that any type of pasta can replace the one demanded by the recipe, in whatever recipe you are preparing. For example, if you wish to make a lasagne, you may use the long lasagne or the small or medium squares, of course, in equal quantity.

Pasta come mostly in the **500 g** package which is surely the most economical and practical size to buy, since pasta have a long shelf life and at any time are ready for a quickly prepared meal enjoyed by most.

How to Peel and Seed Tomatoes

Many tomato recipes to serve on pasta demand that the tomatoes be peeled. Here is the easy way to do it.

Bring some water to boil. It takes 5 minutes at HIGH to boil 4 cups (1 L) of water.

Drop tomatoes two at a time into the boiling water, let stand about 10 seconds. Remove from the boiling water and cool them under running cold water to stop the cooking and facilitate the handling. Cut off the stem with a sharp pointed vegetable knife and peel off the skin. Cut the peeled tomato in half and scoop out the seeds carefully with the fingers. (The seeds give an acid flavor to the tomatoes). They are now ready to use as the recipe demands.

Pasta Cooking Chart

Pasta	Container	Amount of hot water	Approx. time to boil water at HIGH (10) (in minutes)	Approx. time to cook pasta at HIGH (10) (in minutes)	Stand time (in minutes)
Egg Noodles medium width (8 oz - 250 g)	12-cup (3 L) casserole	6 cups (1.5 L)	7 to 8	5 to 6	3
Elbow Macaroni (8 oz - 250 g)	12-cup (3 L) casserole	6 cups (1.5 L)	7 to 8	7 to 8	3
Lasagne Noodles Long or Square (8 oz 125 mL)	12 x 8-inch baking dish	6 cups (1.5 L)	7 to 8	13 to 15	3
Spaghetti (8 oz - 250 g)	12 x 18-inch baking dish	6 cups	8 to 9	7 to 8	3
Specialty Noodles Bows, shells, etc. (8 oz)	12-cup (3 L) casserole	6 cups (1.5 L)	7 to 8	10½ to 11	3

Basic Way to Work with Pasta: Follow directions in above chart for recommended dish size, amount of water and cooking time. Add pasta to boiling water, with 1 teaspoon (5 mL) salt and 1 tablespoon (15 mL) oil.

Microwave, covered, at HIGH (10). Stir twice. Test pasta for doneness and, if necessary, add a little more time. Stir and let stand, covered 3 minutes. Drain, if necessary.

If necessary to reheat after standing time, cover and microwave 1 or 2 minutes at MEDIUM-HIGH.

Assortment of Fresh Pastas →

Monique's Fifteen-Year Pasta
Convection

Monique, my daughter, gave all kinds of amusing names to her creations. Her "Fifteen-Year" I still enjoy. Quickly prepared, yet it has a particular characteristic, the sharp top quality Cheddar cheese, also the fresh basil available in the summer, replaced by the dried type in the winter.

8 oz (227 g) elbow or other macaroni

1 tbsp. (15 mL) vegetable oil

1 19-oz (540 mL) can tomatoes

1 tbsp. (15 mL) basil

1 tsp. (5 mL) sugar

Salt and pepper to taste

1 to 2 cups (250-500 g) strong Cheddar cheese, diced*

2 eggs, beaten

1 cup (250 mL) milk

Microwave macaroni according to How to Cook **Pasta** in the Microwave Oven (see chart).
Drain cooked macaroni, add the oil, stir with a fork until well blended. Place in buttered 8 x 8-inch (20 x 20 cm) microwave-safe dish or 6-cup (1.5 L) dish.
Add the tomatoes, basil, sugar, salt and pepper. Mix the whole with a fork. Stir in the cheese. Stir together the beaten eggs and the milk and pour over the macaroni and cheese.
Preheat the Convection part of your microwave oven 15 minutes at 350°F. (180°C). Set the prepared dish on the oven rack. Bake 40 to 45 minutes or until golden brown on top.

* Use more or less cheese according to your taste

← Top : Dried Fruit Pilaff (p. 28)
← Bottom : Florentine Spinach Filling (p. 74)

Tomato Macaroni
Microwave or Convection

Pour this tasty sauce over cooked macaroni or noodles or any pasta of your choice. There is enough sauce for 1/2 lb (250 g) of cooked pasta. Enjoy!

1 28-oz (796 mL) can tomatoes

1 tsp. (5 mL) sugar

1 tsp. (5 mL) dry mustard

1/2 tsp. (2 mL) pepper

1/2 tsp. (2 mL) each savory and thyme

1 tsp. (5 mL) paprika

1/2 cup (125 mL) celery leaves, minced

1/2 cup (125 mL) tomato paste

1/2 lb (250 g) cooked macaroni

1 cup (250 mL) grated cheese of your choice

1/3 cup (80 mL) fine breadcrumbs

A few spoonfuls of butter or margarine

Butter an 8-cup (2 L) casserole or brush with oil. Mix together the tomatoes, sugar, dry mustard, pepper, thyme, savory, celery leaves, paprika and tomato paste.
Make alternate layers of the tomato mixture, the cooked macaroni and the grated cheese. Sprinkle with the breadcrumbs and dot with butter to taste. Cover dish with waxed paper. Microwave 15 to 20 minutes at MEDIUM or cook in the Convection part of your microwave, preheating the oven 20 minutes at 350°F. (180°C). Set prepared dish on the oven rack and bake 35 to 40 minutes or until top is golden brown.

Old-Fashioned Macaroni
Microwave or Convection

This one is especially good when baked by convection. Do not let the simplicity of this macaroni stop you from making it. You will be surprised at the results. I sometimes mix bits and pieces of leftover cheese.

8 oz (250 g) macaroni of your choice

1/2 lb (250 g) strong Cheddar cheese or any other type of cheese of your choice, grated

3 tbsp. (50 mL) butter

1 cup (250 mL) sour cream

Paprika to taste

Microwave the macaroni according to Pasta Cooking Chart.
Butter a 6-cup (1.5 L) microwave-safe baking dish, place half the cooked macaroni in it, sprinkle with half the cheese, top with half the sour cream and dot with half the butter. Repeat procedure with the remaining ingredients. Sprinkle with paprika. Microwave, uncovered, 8 to 10 minutes at HIGH, or cook in the Convection part of your microwave, preheating the oven 20 minutes at 350°F. (180°C). Set prepared macaroni on the oven rack and bake 20 to 30 minutes or until top is golden.

Delight of the Sea Macaroni Salad

(photo opposite page 17 bottom)

Whether made with canned or fresh or leftover fish, this salad will always be interesting, even for a buffet dish

2 cups (500 mL) cooked macaroni

1 small yellow onion, diced
canned fish*

1 green pepper, diced

1 small red pepper, slivered (optional)

1/2 cup (125 mL) diced celery

3/4 cup (190 mL) commercial sour cream

2 tbsp. (30 mL) light cream or milk

The juice of 1/2 a lemon

1 tbsp. (15 mL) fresh dill, chopped or
1 tsp. (5 mL) dried dill

Microwave the elbow macaroni according to Pasta Cooking Chart. Drain, cool and place in a bowl, add the flaked fish, green and red pepper and diced celery. Stir the whole with a fork.
Blend the remaining ingredients, then mix with the macaroni mixture.
Toss lightly. Serve in a nest of lettuce or surround with watercress. In the summer, I sometimes use the mixture to stuff fresh tomatoes. Do not refrigerate but keep in a cool place until ready to serve.

* Use canned tuna or lobster or a cooked fish of your choice or well-drained canned clams, using the liquid as part of the water to cook the macaroni.

Macaroni Salad "à la Vinaigrette"

A nice easy year-round salad. Serve it in a nest of lettuce or watercress. Decorate the whole with cherry tomatoes.

2 cups (500 mL) cooked macaroni

1 small yellow onion, diced

1/3 cup (80 mL) fresh parsley, minced

1 cucumber, peeled and diced

Dressing:

1/3 cup (80 mL) oil of your choice

1/4 cup (60 mL) fresh lemon juice

1/4 tsp. (2 mL) sugar

1/4 tsp. (2 mL) pepper

1 garlic clove, split in half

1/4 tsp. (1 mL) dry mustard

1 tsp. (5 mL) salt

Place all the Dressing ingredients in a jar. Shake thoroughly before using.*
Cook the macaroni of your choice according to Pasta Cooking Chart. When cooled, add the diced onion, parsley and cucumber. Mix lightly with two forks.
Shake prepared Dressing and add as much as you like over the macaroni mixture. Toss well and place in a nest of greens. Do not refrigerate as it would lose much of its quality.
When tossed with the dressing, this salad will keep 4 to 6 hours at room temperature and will even be tastier for it.

* This dressing will keep for 2 or 3 months at room temperature. Shake well before using. Yield: 1 cup (250 mL).

Sour Cream Macaroni

A meal-in-one. You may wish to add a salad or a cooked vegetable served cold with French dressing.

2 cups (500 mL) macaroni
1 cup (250 mL) grated Cheddar
1 cup (250 mL) cottage cheese
1/2 cup (125 mL) sour cream*

Salt and pepper
4 green onions, minced
2 tbsp. (30 mL) butter

Microwave the macaroni according to the Pasta Cooking Chart. Mix together the Cheddar and cottage cheese. Butter an 8 x 8-inch (20 x 20 cm) baking dish, put half the cooked macaroni in it and sprinkle with half the cheese. Repeat with the remaining macaroni and cheese.
Mix together the sour cream or yogurt, salt, pepper and green onions. To taste, add minced parsley. Dot with butter. Spread over the macaroni. Microwave 8 to 10 minutes at HIGH, uncovered.

* Yogurt may replace the sour cream.

Milanese Macaroni

In Milan, this macaroni is accompanied with a green salad or a bowl of cooked shrimp, served cold in their shell. They are shelled at the table and eaten with a spoonful of hot macaroni.

1 cup (250 mL) macaroni
1 cup (250 mL) grated Cheddar cheese
1/2 tsp. (2 mL) dry mustard

1/4 tsp. (1 mL) fresh ground pepper
1 cup (250 mL) milk
1/2 cup (125 mL) cream of your choice

Microwave the macaroni according to the Pasta Cooking Chart.
Mix together the cheese, mustard and pepper. Butter an 8 x 8-inch (20 x 20 cm) baking dish and fill with layers of the macaroni and of the cheese mixture. Pour the milk and cream over all, mix well. You may, to taste, sprinkle with either paprika, finely minced chives, or 3 to 4 minced green onions or fresh minced parsley. Microwave, uncovered, 10 minutes at MEDIUM-HIGH. Let stand 10 minutes before serving.

Cottage Cheese Macaroni

I like to use the elbow macaroni to make this casserole. If you prefer another type of pasta, simply use an equal quantity of the chosen pasta. In the summer, I use fresh chives and basil from my herb garden.

4 cups (1 L) water	1½ cups (375 mL) cottage cheese
1 medium-sized onion, peeled and cut in two	1/4 cup (60 mL) parsley or chives, chopped fine
1 tsp. (5 mL) salt	2 tbsp. (30 mL) soft butter
2 cups (500 mL) elbow macaroni	1/4 tsp. (1 mL) salt
2 eggs	1/4 tsp. (1 mL) pepper
1 cup (250 mL) milk	1/2 tsp. (2 mL) sweet basil or oregano

Place in a large bowl the water, onion and the teaspoon of salt. Microwave 10 minutes at HIGH. Add the macaroni. Stir and microwave 12 to 14 minutes at HIGH. Strain into a fine sieve. Set aside.

Beat the eggs until light, add the milk and cottage cheese. Mix together with a fork and add the remaining ingredients. Add to the macaroni, stir until the whole is well mixed.

Pour into a well-buttered baking dish. Preheat the convection part of your microwave oven 15 minutes at 350°F. (180°C). Place the dish on a rack. Bake, uncovered, 35 minutes or until golden brown here and there. Serve warm or at room temperature, but not refrigerated.

Noodle and Cottage Cheese Casserole

(photo opposite page 57 top)

A light, most tasty casserole that can easily be prepared in the morning and warmed up for dinner, without losing any of its interesting flavor. Serve with a green salad or a thinly sliced tomato salad.

2 cups (500 mL) noodles of your choice

3/4 cup (190 mL) plain yogurt or sour cream

1 cup (250 mL) cottage cheese

3 tbsp. (50 mL) butter or margarine

Salt and pepper to taste

1/3 cup (80 mL) chopped parsley

3 to 4 green onions, chopped fine

1 egg, lightly beaten

Microwave the noodles in boiling water, according to Pasta Cooking Chart. Drain the cooked noodles and mix in a large bowl with all the remaining ingredients. Toss together with a fork. In the summer, serve at room temperature with a green salad. To serve hot, pour into a microwave-safe, well-buttered dish, microwave 10 minutes at MEDIUM. If not hot enough, microwave another 4 to 5 minutes. According to the type of noodles used, a little more cooking may be required to have them piping hot.

Fried Noodles (Yakisoba)

Cabbage and cooked ham combined with fried noodles make an interesting meal for family and guests. A fried egg can top each portion of noodles before serving.

8 oz (250 g) small egg noodles*

6 cups (1.5 L) water

3 tbsp. (50 mL) vegetable oil

Salt and pepper to taste

3 cups (750 mL) finely shredded cabbage

2 thin slices of cooked ham

1 medium-sized onion, thinly sliced

1 small green pepper, cut into small strips

Sauce:

1/4 cup (60 mL) Ketchup or Chili Sauce

2 tbsp. (30 mL) H.P. Sauce

Bring the water to boil, about 10 minutes at HIGH. Let the noodles fall gently into the water.
Microwave 3 minutes at HIGH. Pour into a large sieve, drain thoroughly.
Pour the oil into a bowl, microwave 1 minute at HIGH. Add the well-drained noodles and stir until they are well coated with the oil. Add salt and pepper to taste. Pour into a dish, cover to keep warm.
Slice the cabbage into thin shreds and do same with the ham, onion and green pepper. Mix together in a bowl.
Microwave another 1 tablespoon (15 mL) of oil 1 minute at MEDIUM-HIGH.
Stir in the vegetable and ham mixture. Microwave 2 minutes at MEDIUM-HIGH. Add to the hot noodles. Mix together the Sauce ingredients, pour over the noodles, stir, microwave 1 minute at HIGH and serve.

* There are different types of small egg noodles to choose from on the market.

Alfredo Special Pasta *(photo opposite page 56)*

Alfredo is one of the famous restaurants in Italy, and his special way to serve "Pasta" is world-renowned. Do not let the simplicity of the dish stop you from making it.

1/2 lb (250 g) fine egg noodles
3/4 cup (190 mL) unsalted butter
1 cup (250 mL) grated Parmesan cheese

Cook the noodles according to Pasta Cooking Chart. Drain, place in a warm dish. Slice the butter over the noodles, microwave 30 seconds at HIGH. Stir to mix the butter, add the grated Parmesan, salt and pepper to taste. Stir again, you will then have a creamy sauce around the noodles. Serve at once.

Côte d'Azur Noodles *(photo opposite page 17 top)*

Pasta of all types are very popular in the South of France. The following recipe is one of my favorites quickly prepared and served with any type of pasta, the choice is yours.

5 cups (1.25 L) cold water
3 cups (750 mL) medium-sized pasta bows*
1 tsp. (5 mL) salt
3/4 cup (190 mL) cooked chicken cut into match sticks

3/4 cup (190 mL) thinly sliced fresh mushrooms
1/2 cup (125 mL) whipping cream
1/2 cup (125 mL) grated Parmesan cheese

Place the cold water in a large 8-cup (2 L) bowl. Microwave 8 minutes at HIGH. Add the pasta and the salt. Stir and microwave 10 minutes at MEDIUM. Drain. Add the remaining ingredients to the hot pasta. Stir well with a fork. Microwave covered 3 minutes at MEDIUM. Stir again and serve.

* Or any other type of pasta.

Pasta Salad "à la Capri" *(photo opposite page 81 top)*

A perfect summer salad when tomatoes and basil are abundant and fragrant. In Capri, Italy, it is referred to as **"Penne a la Capresa".** It is a great summer delight to serve this uncooked cold sauce over the hot pasta. Try it, it is a delightful experience.

4 large tomatoes

**3 tbsp. (50 mL) fresh basil leaves or
  2 tsp. (10 mL) dried basil leaves**

2 garlic cloves, chopped fine

1/2 tsp. (2 mL) sugar

Salt and pepper to taste

A few spoonfuls of olive oil*

1-lb (500 g) box vermicelli

1 cup (250 mL) grated cheese**

Peel and dice the tomatoes into 1/2-inch (1.25 cm) pieces, place in a bowl and add the basil, garlic, sugar, salt and pepper. Mix gently, add the olive oil. Leave on kitchen counter to marinate for 1 to 2 hours. The flavors will mix and juice will form.

When ready to serve, cook vermicelli according to Pasta Cooking Chart. Drain well, pour into a serving bowl and add the tomato mixture, stir to mix the whole, top with the grated cheese. Serve as soon as ready.

* *Use any oil of your choice.*
** *I prefer the fresh grated Mozzarella cheese, but if it is not readily available you may use the cheese you prefer. A good mild Cheddar is my preferred type to replace the Mozzarella.*

Summer Stars

So called because it is prepared with tiny star pasta and a super fresh parsley sauce. I like to serve my **summer stars** when the fresh parsley in my garden is in full bloom.

1/2 cup (125 mL) each butter and margarine	**1/2 cup (125 mL) grated Parmesan cheese**
1 large garlic clove, chopped fine	**2 or 3 cups (500 or 750 mL) stars or any**
1 cup (250 mL) fresh chopped parsley	**small pasta of your choice**

Place the butter and margarine in a bowl. Microwave 2 minutes at HIGH. Add the garlic, microwave another minute at HIGH. Add the parsley and the cheese. Stir to mix. Set aside.
Bring 4 cups (1 L) water to boil, 5 minutes at HIGH, add the pasta, cover and microwave 6 to 7 minutes, let stand until ready to serve. It will remain hot for 10 to 15 minutes. Drain, if necessary, add to the cheese mixture, stir well and serve. Excellent served as a vegetable.

Leeks and Shells "à la Parisienne"

All over France during mid-summer, when fresh leeks are at their luscious best, the French make a very simple leek sauce to serve over hot noodles and serve with grated Swiss cheese.

3 to 4 leeks	**3 cups (750 mL) small egg noodle shells***
1/3 cup (80 mL) butter	**Grated cheese of your choice**
Salt and pepper to taste	

Clean leeks and cut them, the white and most of the green, in 1/2-inch (1 cm) lengths.
Melt the butter 3 minutes at HIGH in a 6-cup dish. Add the leeks, stir until well buttered. Let stand.
To cook the small egg noodle shells, measure 6 cups (1.5 L) water in a large dish. Microwave 6 minutes at HIGH. Add the noodles. Microwave 5 minutes at HIGH. Drain, add to the melted leeks. Stir well, add salt and pepper to taste. Microwave 1 minute à HIGH. Serve as soon as ready, with a bowl of grated cheese.

* The shells and leeks can be cooked a few hours ahead of time, stirred together, covered and warmed up 4 minutes at MEDIUM-HIGH when ready to serve. Stir well after 2 minutes of cooking.

Monique's Meatless Lasagne *(photo opposite page 57 bottom)*

Microwave and Convection

A large recipe to serve 10 to 12, or you may make it in 2 dishes, freeze one and serve the other. Use the frozen one within 6 to 8 weeks. A large plastic bowl is required to cook the noodles or cook two batches. To make it with meat, follow instructions given in the recipe.

20 cups (2.5 L) water

1 tbsp. (15 mL) salt

1 tbsp. (15 mL) vegetable oil

1 box (500 g) lasagne noodles

2 lb (1 kg) cottage cheese

1 cup (250 mL) commercial sour cream

2 eggs

1/2 tsp. (2 mL) each pepper and oregano

1 lb (500 g) Mozzarella cheese, thinly sliced

3 tbsp. (50 mL) vegetable oil

2 large onions, chopped fine

1/4 cup (60 mL) diced celery

1 28-oz (796 mL) can tomatoes

2 6-oz (260 mL) cans tomato paste

1/4 tsp. (1 mL) pepper

1 tsp. (5 mL) basil

2 tsp. (10 mL) sugar

2 10-oz (384 mL) cans mushroom stems and pieces

and/or

1½ lb (750 g) ground beef

Pour water into a large bowl, add the salt and the vegetable oil. Microwave at HIGH 10 to 12 minutes. Place lasagne noodles one by one in the water. Microwave at HIGH 10 minutes, test for tenderness with a fork or the point of a knife. Depending on the brand, it could take 5 to 9 minutes more for the lasagne to become tender. Place the container in the sink, let cold water drip over the whole until the noodles have cooled. Drain.

Meanwhile, mix the cottage cheese, sour cream, eggs, pepper and oregano with salt to taste.

Butter a large oblong baking dish or two 8 x 8-inch (20 x 20 cm) dishes. Separate the slices of Mozzarella cheese. Microwave 2 tablespoons (30 mL) of the oil in a dish 4 minutes at HIGH. Add the onions and the celery, microwave 2 minutes at HIGH, stir well and microwave 2 minutes more at HIGH, the onions should then be golden brown here and there. Strain the tomatoes to remove the seeds, pressing down the pulp through the sieve, then add to the onions and celery, stir and add the tomato paste, pepper, basil and sugar.

When using ground meat, heat the remaining tablespoons of vegetable oil in a dish 1 minute at HIGH, add the ground beef to the hot oil. Salt and pepper to taste, microwave at MEDIUM-HIGH 2 minutes, stir well with a fork to break up the meat, microwave another 2 minutes at MEDIUM-HIGH. Add to the onion and celery mixture. Taste for seasoning.

To prepare the lasagne, place a layer of the cooked noodles in long strips to cover the bottom of the dish, top with a layer of the creamed cheese mixture, then the slices of Mozzarella, then the sauce, repeat these layers until dish is filled, ending up with noodles, sauce and topping of sliced cheese.

Whatever the size of the dish, bake uncovered in the convection part of your microwave preheated 10 minutes at 325°F. (160°C) for 1 hour 15 minutes per dish.

When ready to serve, if prepared ahead of time, place the lasagne on a rack in the microwave and reheat 10 minutes at MEDIUM for each dish. Serve.

Rice and Noodle Pilaff

Fine noodles and quick cooking rice, combined and cooked together, result in a tasty casserole that can be served with roast chicken or pork, but also elegant served as a vegetarian dish for a buffet or a light lunch.

This pilaff is a classic of the Armenian Cuisine.

4 tbsp. (60 mL) butter or margarine

1/2 cup (125 mL) fine noodles or small pasta shells

1 cup (250 mL) quick cooking rice

1 tsp. (5 mL) salt

2 cups (500 mL) hot chicken broth or hot water

Melt the butter or margarine 3 minutes at HIGH in a 4-cup (1 L) microwave-safe dish. Add the fine noodles or pasta shells and the quick cooking rice. Stir together until both are well buttered.

Add the salt and the hot chicken broth or water. Stir, microwave, uncovered, 6 minutes at HIGH. According to the type of pasta used, it is sometimes necessary to microwave 1 or 2 minutes more or less. This is a sort of basic recipe which lends itself to many variations.

Variation 1: Add to the pilaff, when cooked, 1 cup (250 mL) more or less of canned peas. I use the water drained from the peas as part of the liquid to cook he pilaff.

Variation 2: Dice an unpeeled tomato, sprinkle with a good pinch of sugar and basil to taste. Microwave 1 minute at HIGH, add to pilaff when adding the butter. Stir well and finish cooking as in the recipe.

Variation 3: Slice thinly 1/2 pound (250 g) fresh mushrooms, 2 green onions. Melt 1 tablespoon (15 mL) butter in a dish, add the mushrooms and green onions. Stir well. Microwave 1 minute at HIGH. Pour over the rice and noodle pilaff just before cooking it. Stir well and microwave according to time given for pilaff.

Note: When chives and parsley are readily available in the summer, add 1/4 cup (60 mL) of each to the hot pasta. Stir with a fork until well blended.

Chopped Beef Noodle Casserole

This casserole will give you ten servings, but as I find it is just as easy to make the whole recipe, when cooked, I divide it in two, one half to serve, the other half to place in a freezer dish and freeze. I then have an emergency casserole which can go from the freezer to my microwave oven, to defrost and warm up when needed, which takes about 10 minutes at DEFROST, 10 minutes at MEDIUM-HIGH to heat up.

2 tbsp. (30 mL) butter or margarine

1 large onion, peeled and chopped

1 cup (250 mL) diced celery

1 large garlic clove, chopped fine

1 lb (500 g) ground beef

1 10-oz (284 mL) can sliced mushrooms, undrained

1 7½-oz (213 mL) can tomato sauce

1/2 cup (250 mL) chicken consommé or water

1 tsp. (5 mL) salt

Pepper to taste

The grated rind of a lemon

1 tsp. (5 mL) lemon juice

8 oz (250 g) egg noodles

1 cup (250 mL) grated Cheddar cheese

Microwave noodles according to Pasta Cooking Chart.
Combine butter or margarine and onion in a large microwave-safe casserole. Microwave at HIGH 1 minute, stir and add the celery and garlic, microwave at HIGH 1 minute. Stir well, add crumbled ground beef, stir to mix the whole, microwave at HIGH 5 minutes. Stir well and add the remaining ingredients except the cheese. Mix thoroughly. Cover and microwave at HIGH 10 minutes, stir, add the cheese, stir until well blended, microwave at MEDIUM 10 minutes. Serve.

Japanese Noodles

In Japan, "Menrui" or noodles are eaten winter or summer.

They are served either very hot, in special broths, or very cold, with different types of dipping sauces or garnishes. There are different types, easily available in our part of the world, in shops specializing in Japanese imports. The UDON type are slim, white or wholewheat noodles, that cook in a minute or two in boiling liquid, to be served over hot vegetables, superb with chicken. The HIYAMUGI noodles are a medium-sized wheat noodle usually served cold on a bed of finely crushed ice, with a cold dipping sauce.

I love those served cold with steamed shrimp or scallops, hot or cold. I also enjoy the cold cooked noodles topped with chopped cold hard boiled eggs.

If you wish to serve a choice of flavoring or seasoning with any type of the cooked noodles, try peeled and grated fresh ginger to taste, add to chopped green onions, super with roast chicken, or served with seafood.

add to toasted sesame seeds with lamb stew or roast

add to chopped watercress to serve with steak,

add to chopped watercress tossed with a tablespoon of salad oil to serve with fish.

With all types of cooked chicken, toss with fine cooked noodles, grated ginger to taste and 2 tablespoons (30 mL) of Sake (rice wine). Instead of Sake, I like to use Mirin, which is a sweet rice wine, also available in Japanese food shops. Super served with cooked shrimp and Japanese soy sauce, the best one being KIKKOMAN Soy Sauce.

Eggs

Alfredo Special Pasta (p. 47) →

Eggs

Who is not aware that eggs are essential in custards, omelets, mousses, mayonnaise, etc. or to bind meat loaves, or for the golden, tender quality of cakes, or on the crust for pastry, or to clarify consommé, for breakfast, lunch or dinner. But, what to me is still more interesting about eggs are the 1001 different dishes in which eggs are an essential ingredient, and yet there are but a few basic methods to use or cook them.

Some people won't buy eggs with yellow shells, others, eggs with white shells; the color of an eggshell is determined by the breed of hens and has absolutely nothing to do with the flavor or quality of the egg.

Cooking Eggs in the Microwave

You really have to be knowledgeable to cook eggs in the microwave. If you follow the different ways which I have used for the last three years, you will soon learn all about cooking eggs in the microwave, and sucessfully, to be sure.

There could be **seconds** of difference to what is given in the recipe, according to the type of eggs you buy, small, medium or large. Whether they are refrigerated on open shelves or in their closed box, the cold in the eggs can differ and change the cooking time by one or two seconds.

Three Important Rules

- **Do not ever** microwave a whole egg in the shell, since the egg is sure to explode and make a mess in your oven.

  Do not try to reheat a hard cooked egg in its shell, for the same reason as above, but it can be peeled and placed in a bowl, covered with hot water to the top, microwaved 30 seconds at HIGH.

- **When cooking whole any type of egg,** fried, poached, etc., in the microwave, make 2 or 3 invisible holes in the white and the yolk with the point of a small knife which breaks the invisible skin covering the egg and prevents it from exploding in the oven, not dangerous but messy.

  I strongly advise against cooking eggs, boiled, poached, or as an omelet at HIGH. Medium power (50%) is the best.

  If your oven has only one power, which would be HIGH, place a 2-cup (500 mL) measure of cold water in the microwave alongside the egg. The water will absorb some of the microwaves.

  Another important factor to be aware of: the high fat content of the yolk makes it cook faster than the white, which is the reverse of the conventional way.

- If you wish to have microwaved egg yolks remain soft, remove the dish from the microwave before the whites are completely cooked. Cover with waxed paper and let stand 1 to 2 minutes. They will not get cold, but just firm as they should be.

When Frying Bacon Before Cooking the Eggs, there are two ways to proceed:

1) If you do not wish to keep the melted fat, place the bacon slices one next to the other on a piece of white towelling paper on the serving plate. Microwave 1 to 3 slices 20 to 30 seconds, according to how you like your bacon. Remove the greasy paper and set aside while cooking the eggs.

2) If you wish to keep the fat, microwave the bacon on a smaller plate without paper. As soon as done place the fat in a jar and keep refrigerated. When the egg is cooked, place the hot bacon around it.

← Top : Noodle and Cottage Cheese Casserole (p. 46)
← Bottom : Monique's Meatless Lasagne (p. 50)

Bacon and Eggs

A favorite breakfast for so many, taking a minute or so to prepare directly on one's plate or in the **Browning Pan.**

1, 2 or 3 slices of bacon
1 or 2 eggs
Parsley or chives to taste

There are two ways to proceed with the bacon (See beginning of chapter **When frying bacon before cooking the eggs,** page 57).
When the bacon is cooked, remove from plate, break the egg into the plate, one or two as you prefer. Pierce the yolk and the white of the egg 2 to 3 times with the point of a knife (See Fried Eggs below). Microwave 1 egg 20 to 25 seconds, 2 eggs 25 to 35 seconds to 1 minute, the time depends on individual taste, just as for fried eggs. Add the cooked bacon and serve.

Fried Eggs

Quick and easy to prepare. Cooked in a small plate, the egg will have no color, but if you use a marvellous small **Browning Pan** (Corning), you can control the color of the butter while making a parfect fried egg or two at a time.

1 tsp. (5 mL) butter or bacon fat
1 egg
Salt and pepper to taste

If you use the small **Browning Pan,** melt in it the butter or bacon fat 30 to 40 seconds at HIGH. Break the egg into the melted fat. Pierce the yolk and the white gently with the point of a knife, 3 to 4 times. Microwave at MEDIUM-HIGH 25 to 30 seconds. The difference in time depends on the size of the egg. To fry 2 eggs, the procedure is the same, simply microwave 10 to 20 seconds more to melt the fat and cook the eggs.

Scrambled Eggs

If you need more than one or two eggs for the same service, this is a good easy way to prepare them.

4 eggs
1/4 tsp. (1 mL) salt
1/4 cup (60 mL) light cream or milk
2 tbsp. (30 mL) butter

Break the eggs into a bowl, add the salt and cream or milk, and beat with a fork, just enough to blend. Melt the butter in a glass or ceramic pie plate 2 minutes at HIGH, it will be golden brown. Pour the beaten eggs into the hot butter. Microwave 1 minute at MEDIUM. Stir gently and microwave another minute if necessary. The easy way is to pour the soft portion over the partly cooked portion and move lightly with a fork. According to how cold the eggs and liquid were, it could take a few more seconds of cooking, remembering that even after 2 minutes out of the Microwave oven, the eggs will keep on cooking.

Poached Eggs

If you prefer to eat eggs without any type of fat, poached eggs are perfect and easy to cook in the microwave.

1/2 cup (125 mL) water
1/4 tsp. (1 mL) vinegar or lemon juice
1 egg

Place in a small dish or a teacup, the water, vinegar or lemon juice. Microwave 2 minutes at HIGH. Break the egg into a saucer, pierce the yolk and the white of the egg with the point of a knife, then gently pour the egg into the hot water. Microwave at MEDIUM 40 to 50 seconds, depending whether you like it more or less cooked. Remove egg from the water with a slotted spoon, place it on buttered toast or on an English muffin cut in half. In the summer, try sprinkling the egg or the toast with chives.

Notes: To poach 2 eggs at a time, heat 2 cups (500 mL) water 7 to 8 minutes at HIGH. Pierce the yolk and the white of the eggs with the point of a knife, microwave the 2 eggs together 1 minute at MEDIUM-HIGH. Cover and let stand 1 minute. Serve. I do not advise poaching more than 2 eggs at a time, as some parts will be overcooked, others undercooked.

Mushroom Poached Eggs *(photo opposite page 64)*

I always keep a can of condensed mushroom soup on the shelf and some English muffins in my freezer, so if an emergency arises I am ready to present in a few minutes **My Speed-Cooked Eggs,** which are poached eggs topped with a mushroom sauce.

2 tbsp. (30 mL) butter	4 eggs
1 can condensed cream of mushroom soup	Salt and pepper to taste
1/3 cup (80 mL) milk or white wine	2 English muffins, toasted and buttered

Melt the butter 1 minute at HIGH in a ceramic or Pyrex pie plate. Add the soup and the milk or wine. Stir well. Microwave at MEDIUM-HIGH 2 minutes, or until sauce is hot, stirring once.

Break the eggs, one at a time, into a small plate, make an incision once in the yolks, once in the whites, with the point of a knife. Gently slide the eggs into the creamy sauce, one by one, until all 4 are in the hot sauce. Then, with a spoon, carefully pour some of the hot sauce here and there over the eggs. Salt and pepper. Cover with waxed paper. Microwave 3 minutes at HIGH. Check doneness of the eggs.

To serve, place one egg with some of the sauce on one half of the English muffin, toasted and buttered.

Note: In the summer, I sprinkle the butter with minced chives; in winter, I use fresh parsley or dried tarragon.

Baked Eggs and Cheese *(photo opposite page 33 top)*

A simple, easy quick way to make a good breakfast, or light supper. Serve with toast and a watercress salad. These eggs are baked in custard cups.

4 thin slices of the cheese of your choice	1/4 tsp. (1 mL) curry powder
4 eggs	2 tsp. (10 mL) sherry or Madeira
1/4 cup (60 mL) Chili sauce	Minced chives or parsley to taste

Line each ramekin with a slice of cheese. Break an egg on top of each slice of cheese. Pierce the white and the yolk of each egg with the point of a knife.

Mix together the Chili sauce, curry powder, sherry or Madeira. Divide equally over each egg.

Microwave 2 ramekins at a time 40 to 45 seconds at MEDIUM. Let stand on kitchen counter covered with waxed paper, while you microwave the other two also 40 to 45 seconds at MEDIUM.

Baked Eggs à la Française

Serve for a light lunch or supper. My favorite way to serve these is topped with fresh minced chives. For a light meal, serve with a salad and a poached fruit (see Dessert book) for dessert. These are very elegant when baked and served in ceramic ramekins.

2 eggs

2 tsp. (10 mL) milk or cream

1 tsp. (5 mL) butter

Salt and pepper to taste

Minced parsley or chives

To make these, use glass custard cups or French ceramic ramekins. Break eggs into ramekins, one egg in each. Pierce the yolks and the whites carefully with the point of a little knife. Pour 1 teaspoon (5 mL) of milk or cream over each egg. Place the 2 dishes in the microwave oven. Microwave at MEDIUM 35 to 40 seconds. Depending on the power of your oven or the size of the eggs, the cooking may take 10 to 12 seconds more. To check, simply look and touch the white part of the eggs. To taste, top with the minced parsley or chives and serve.

Omelette Fermière

Quick and easy to prepare. The ham can be replaced by bacon. Serve with buttered noodles or cooked potatoes for a light meal.

3 eggs	2 tbsp. (30 mL) minced parsley
3 tbsp. (50 mL) milk	A thin slice of ham
Salt and pepper to taste	2 tsp. (10 mL) butter

Beat the eggs and milk together, salt and pepper to taste, add the parsley and stir thoroughly.
Dice the ham, removing fat if any. Stir into the beaten eggs.
Melt 1 teaspoon (5 mL) of the butter in an 8-inch (20 cm) ceramic or Pyrex pie plate 1 minute at HIGH. Pour in the omelet mixture. Cover with plastic wrap. Microwave 30 seconds at HIGH, lift wrap, gently stir the cooked part of the omelet, allowing the uncooked part to flow under. Cover again, microwave at MEDIUM 1 minute 10 seconds. Let stand 1 minute and serve.

Scandinavian Omelet *(photo opposite page 33 bottom)*

A light, fluffy 3-egg omelet, filled with salmon, green onions and dill. The salmon is sometimes replaced by an equal quantity of chopped cooked shrimp.

3 eggs, separated	1/2 cup (125 mL) cooked salmon
2 tbsp. (30 mL) milk or water	4 green onions, chopped fine
1 tbsp. (15 mL) butter	1 tsp. (5 mL) dill, chopped fine

Whip the egg whites until they form soft peaks. Beat the egg yolks with the milk or water. Gently fold the whites into the yolks.
Melt the butter in a 9-inch (22.5 cm) Pyrex or Corning pie plate, 1 minute at HIGH. Pour the eggs into the hot butter. Pierce the whites and the yolks with the point of a knife. Microwave at MEDIUM 3 to 4 minutes or until eggs are set.
While the eggs are cooking, mix together the cooked salmon, green onions and dill. Pour over the cooked omelet. Fold in half and serve.

My Favorite 3-Egg Omelet

You can serve this omelet just as is or with a filling of your choice, or one of the following variations. It is easy and quick to make.

3 eggs

3 tbsp. (50 mL) sour cream

Salt and pepper to taste

Break the eggs in a bowl, add the sour cream, salt and pepper. Butter generously a 9-inch (22.5 cm) ceramic pie plate and pour in the egg mixture. Cover with waxed paper. Microwave 2 minutes at MEDIUM. Stir lightly, moving the outer portions of the omelet to the center of the plate, microwave another 2 minutes at MEDIUM.

Place your choice of filling or sauce in the middle, fold the omelet over. Microwave 30 seconds more at MEDIUM-LOW. Serve.

Fillings for Omelets

There is a great variety of fillings for omelets.

See how to proceed to make the omelet according to the method given in **My Favorite 3-Egg Omelet.**

Albertans' Favorite Omelet

1 tsp. (5 mL) butter or bacon fat

1/2 cup (125 mL) diced cooked ham

A small onion, chopped fine

1/4 cup (60 mL) slivered red or green pepper

Melt the butter or bacon fat in a 1-cup (250 mL) glass measure or a bowl, 1 minute at HIGH. Add the ham, onion and red or green pepper. Stir well, microwave 2 minutes at HIGH, stirring once. Salt and pepper to taste, add a small pinch of sugar.

Make the omelet according to the method given in **My Favorite 3-Egg Omelet.**

Swiss Mountain Special Omelet

Fresh mushrooms and Swiss or mild Cheddar cheese, used to garnish this omelet, make it quite special.

1 cup (250 mL) fresh mushrooms, sliced

1/4 cup (60 mL) green onions, chopped fine

2 tbsp. (30 mL) butter

Salt and pepper to taste

1/2 cup (125 mL) grated Swiss or mild Cheddar cheese

Place in a bowl the fresh mushrooms, green onions and butter. Cover and microwave 2 minutes at HIGH. Stir well. Salt and pepper to taste.

Make **My Favorite 3-Egg Omelet,** fill it with the mushroom and green onions mixture. Top with the grated cheese. Serve.

"Fines-herbes" Omelet (photo opposite page 72)

In the summer, when you have fresh herbs available in your garden or at the Farmers' Market, try this omelet. I grow my herbs, so as soon as they are ready, I make sure to have my first "Fines-Herbes" Omelet for lunch, which I serve with hot French bread and a salad.

A 3-egg omelet (See My Favorite 3-Egg Omelet)

3 tbsp. (50 mL) chopped parsley

2 tbsp. (30 mL) fresh chives, chopped fine

1 tbsp. (15 mL) chopped basil

1 tbsp. (15 mL) chopped dill

Prepare the omelet, adding to the egg mixture, the parsley, chives, basil and dill. Stir until well mixed. Microwave as indicated in the recipe. Serve.

Omelet "à la Reine"

A classic way of the French Cuisine to serve an omelet. Excellent even when using leftover chicken. Serve with a green salad or hot buttered spinach.

2 tbsp. (30 mL) butter

1 cup (250 mL) slivered leftover cooked chicken

1/2 tsp. (2 mL) dried tarragon

A 3-egg omelet (see My Favorite 3-Egg Omelet)

Melt the butter 1 minute at HIGH in a 9-inch (22.5 cm) pie plate. Add the chicken, stir well. Add the tarragon, salt and pepper to taste. Stir again, cover and microwave 2 minutes at MEDIUM. Prepare the omelet. When cooked, fill with the chicken, fold and top, to taste, with the plain Sauce Velouté (see sauce chapter), also flavored with a bit of tarragon.

Chicken Liver Omelet

Another sure success whenever I serve this omelet. Enjoy it with a bowl of fresh crisp watercress.

2 tbsp. (30 mL) margarine or butter

1/2 lb (250 g) fresh chicken liver, slivered

1 tsp. (5 mL) flour

2 tbsp. (30 mL) sherry of your choice

Salt and pepper to taste

3 green onions, chopped fine

A 3-egg omelet (see My Favorite 3-Egg Omelet)

Place the butter or margarine in a 9-inch (22.5 cm) pie plate. Microwave 2 minutes at HIGH (the butter must sizzle). Add the slivered chicken liver. Stir well. Sprinkle with the flour, salt and pepper to taste. Microwave 2 minutes at MEDIUM. Add the sherry and the green onions. Microwave 2 minutes at MEDIUM.

Make the omelet. Garnish with the hot chicken liver mixture.

Mushroom Poached Eggs (p. 60) →

Spanish Omelet *(photo opposite page 65 bottom)*

For a perfect Spanish Omelet, fresh tomatoes are a must, and without them I would not consider making the omelet. This is an interesting light luncheon dish served with a bowl of watercress or a rice salad, followed by poached fruit, in season. Very Spanish! Excellent for the weight watcher.

1 tbsp. (15 mL) olive or vegetable oil

1/2 green pepper, chopped fine

2 to 4 green onions, chopped fine

1/4 cup (60 mL) celery, diced

A good pinch of thyme

2 fresh unpeeled tomatoes, diced

1 tsp. (5 mL) sugar

1/2 tsp. (2 mL) salt

3 tbsp. (50 mL) fresh chopped parsley

A 3-egg omelet (See *My Favorite 3-Egg Omelet*)

Place the oil in a ceramic or Pyrex pie plate and microwave 1 minute at HIGH. Add the green pepper, onions, celery and thyme. Microwave 4 minutes at MEDIUM-HIGH, stirring once.
Add the tomatoes, sugar, salt and parsley, mix well, cover and microwave 2 minutes at HIGH, let stand 5 minutes.
In the meantime, prepare the omelet, pour over the vegetables and serve.

Hua Eggs in Red Sauce

Spanish poached Eggs topped with a quickly made tomato sauce.

3 tbsp. (50 mL) olive or vegetable oil

2 small onions, chopped fine

1 garlic clove, minced

1 16-oz (454 g) can tomatoes

1 tbsp. (15 mL) minced parsley

1/2 tsp. (2 mL) each salt and marjoram

1/4 tsp. (1 mL) each pepper and sugar

4 to 6 eggs

Pour the oil into a Corning Browning Dish, microwave 2 minutes at HIGH, add the onions and garlic, stir well. Microwave 2 minutes at HIGH, stirring once, add the tomatoes, parsley, salt, marjoram, pepper and sugar.
Microwave 6 minutes at HIGH, stirring once after 4 minutes.
Break the eggs one at a time into a small dish, then slip the eggs one by one into the hot sauce, spooning a bit of sauce gently over each egg. Cover and microwave at MEDIUM 1 minute per egg.
An elegant way to serve them is to tast split English muffins or bread of your choice, lift a poached egg onto each toast with a perforated spoon, pour sauce over all.

← Top : Brown Rice Salad (p. 32)
← Bottom : Spanish Omelet (above)

Rolled Omelet

(Tamago Yaki)

Simple and quick to make when using the microwave oven. If you are dieting, this recipe will give you a very nourishing, nonfattening dish.

2 green onions, finely chopped

4 eggs

2 tsp. (10 mL) Japanese soy sauce

2 tbsp. (30 mL) vegetable oil

1 small cucumber

Beat together with a fork the green onions, eggs and soy sauce.

Pour 1 tablespoon (15 mL) of the oil into an 8-inch (20 cm) pie plate, microwave 1 minute at HIGH. Pour half the egg mixture into the hot plate, quickly spread mixture into a thin coating covering the bottom of the plate. Microwave at MEDIUM 40 seconds. Roll up the omelet, slip into a warm plate. Repeat for the other half of the mixture.

I sometimes cut 6 cooked and shelled shrimp into thin slices which I divide evenly over each omelet before folding.

Cheese Omelet

This omelette is made in a Browning Dish.

4 eggs

1/4 cup (60 mL) milk

1/4 tsp. (1 mL) salt

A dash of pepper

2 tsp. (10 mL) butter

1/2 cup (125 mL) grated cheese

Combine eggs, milk, salt and pepper in a medium-sized bowl; beat until well blended.

Heat a Browning Dish for 3 minutes at HIGH. Place butter in the Browning Dish, when melted, add the egg mixture. Cover with lid or waxed paper and microwave at MEDIUM 3 to 3½ minutes or until almost set in the centre. Sprinkle with cheese, cover and let stand for 2 minutes.

Loosen eggs with rubber spatula, tilt Browning Dish and roll omelette onto serving plate.

How to Make an Omelet
in a Browning Dish

If you have a Browning Dish (Corning), here is the way to make an omelet that will be brown under when folded, just as if it had been cooked in a frying pan.

2 eggs, lightly beaten

2 tbsp. (30 mL) milk, cream or water

1/2 tsp. (2 mL) salt

2 tsp. (10 mL) butter

Place the Browning Dish in the microwave oven. Microwave 3 minutes at HIGH.
Mix in a bowl, the eggs, milk, cream or water and salt.
Place the butter in the hot Browning Dish, it will sizzle and brown in just a few second. Swirl the melted butter so as to cover all the bottom of the dish. Pour in the eggs beaten with the remaining ingredients. Microwave 1 minute at MEDIUM-HIGH. If necessary, push the cooked part of the omelet to the middle of the dish and microwave 30 to 35 seconds more at MEDIUM. Serve as is or top with any garnish or sauce you like.

Sausages, Eggs and Hashed Brown

The good old-fashioned English breakfast. To our way of eating today, it can be an interesting lunch or light dinner. For perfect results in the browning, I recommend using a preheated Browning Dish.

2 medium-sized potatoes	2 green onions, chopped fine
1/2 lb (250 g) sausages	3 to 4 eggs
1/4 tsp. (1 mL) paprika	Salt and pepper to taste

Scrub potatoes and pierce skin 2 to 3 times with the point of a knife. Microwave 5 minutes at HIGH. Set aside.

Sprinkle sausages with paprika. When using Browning Dish, preheat 6 minutes at HIGH. Add the prepared sausages to the hot dish without removing it from the oven. Microwave 3 minutes at HIGH. Shake pan or stir sausages and microwave 2 minutes at HIGH. Place sausages on serving dish. While sausages are cooking, peel and dice the baked potatoes, sprinkle with paprika, salt and pepper to taste and toss with the green onions, mix well and add to the remaining fat in the Browning Dish, stir well and microwave 3 minutes at HIGH, stirring once. Place potatoes around the edge of the dish. Set sausages on top of the potatoes.

Break the eggs into a soup plate and set in the middle of the Browning Dish, cover with waxed paper or a lid. Microwave at MEDIUM about 4 minutes or until the eggs are cooked to the degree of doneness you prefer.

Quiche Lorraine *(photo opposite page 80)*

Microwave or Convection

The classic quiche is prepared with diced bacon or salt pork and Swiss cheese. Here is my favorite version, using diced bacon or salt pork and mild or strong Cheddar cheese. To taste, omit the pie crust, simply pour the mixture directly into the plate. Cook as indicated.

Lard pie crust	1/2 tsp. (2 mL) salt
6 slices bacon or salt pork, diced	1/4 tsp. (1 mL) pepper
3 eggs	1/4 tsp. (1 mL) nutmeg
1 cup (250 mL) heavy cream	1 cup (250 mL) grated Cheddar cheese

Cut the bacon or salt pork into 1-inch (2.5 cm) pieces. Place a sheet of towelling over a plate and place the diced bacon or salt pork on it. Microwave 2 or 3 minutes at HIGH.

Beat together in a bowl, the eggs, cream, salt, pepper and nutmeg. Add the grated cheese. Mix together. Line a pie plate with the rolled dough*. Spread the diced bacon or salt pork over the crust and pour the cheese mixture over all. To taste, sprinkle with a little grated cheese.

Microwave 8 to 9 minutes at MEDIUM or preheat the convection part of your microwave oven at 400°F. (200°C) 20 minutes. Place the prepared quiche on the oven rack and bake 30 minutes. Check for doneness with the point of a knife. Serve hot or tepid.

* To microwave the quiche, precook the crust 3 minutes at HIGH. Cool before filling with the cheese mixture.

Egg Wisdom

The egg has under its shell "What we all need to keep us healthy and well".
Treat it accordingly. Easy to do when you are aware of a few basic facts.
- The egg, inside its shell, is bursting with vitamins, good for young and old.
- Microwave eggs at MEDIUM, MEDIUM-LOW or LOW.
- Eggs do not have to be just eggs: a poached egg on toast is a nourishing, tasty meal, served on a thin
  slice of ham, a man's favorite, topped with Hollandaise sauce it becomes an elegant dish, and so forth. Try
  some of the following egg recipes. I hope they will give you an inspiration to adapt your own favorites to
  microwave cooking.
- Keep eggs cool, by placing them in the refrigerator, preferably out of the box.
- It does not matter if the shell is brown or white, all that counts is freshness.
  You will find it very easy to separate the white from the yolk when the eggs are cold.
- Do not wash eggs before placing them in the refrigerator, as they have a protective coating that
  will help keep them fresh until ready to use.
- To obtain a good fluffy volume when beating egg whites, let stand 20 to 30 minutes at room temperature
  before beating.
- Egg whites keep for weeks when stored in a well covered jar (jam jars are perfect) and refrigerated.
- It does not matter whether the shell is brown or white, what counts is freshness. I hope you will find the
  recipes in this chapter an incentive to prepare eggs the easy microwave way.

Sauces

"Fines-herbes" Omelet (p. 64) →

Favorite Sauces to Serve with Eggs

Basic White Sauce and Variations

2 tbsp. (30 mL) butter or bacon fat
2 tbsp. (30 mL) flour

1 cup (250 mL) milk or consommé
Salt and pepper to taste

Melt butter 40 seconds at HIGH, add the flour, stir until well mixed. Add the milk or consommé. Stir, microwave at HIGH 2 minutes. Stir well, season to taste. Microwave another minute at MEDIUM, if necessary.

Variations:
Cheese Sauce: To Basic White Sauce, add 1/4 teaspoon (1 mL) dry mustard, 1/2 cup (125 mL) grated cheese of your choice.
Mushroom Sauce: Melt 1 tablespoon (15 mL) butter 1 minute at HIGH, add 1 cup (250 mL) thinly sliced mushrooms, stir until mushrooms are coated with the melted butter. Add 1 or 2 green onions thinly sliced. Mix well, add to 1 cup (250 mL) milk or chicken consommé. Stir and microwave 4 minutes at MEDIUM-HIGH, stirring once during the cooking period. Season to taste.
Tomato Sauce or Spanish Red Sauce· To Basic White Sauce, add 3 tablespoons (50 mL) tomato purée or paste (the purée is lighter than the paste, but more difficult to find). Mix and microwave 2 minutes at HIGH.
Curry Sauce: To Basic White Sauce, add 1/2 to 1 teaspoon (2 to 5 mL) curry powder, 1 diced green onion, stir well and microwave 2 minutes at MEDIUM.
Dill Sauce: To Basic White Sauce, add 1 or 2 tablespoons (15 to 30 mL) fresh or dried dill plus a dash of nutmeg. Mix well and microwave 2 minutes at MEDIUM.

← Top : Cheese Rice Ring (p. 30)
← Bottom : Wild Rice Vegetable Casserole (p. 32)

Sauces to serve on Omelets

There are so many ways to vary an omelet that there is no excuse for serving it forever in the same manner. I hope you will be tempted by the following ideas.

Velouté Sauce for Omelets

To this basic sauce, you may add melted leeks or green onions or cooked spinach, chopped fresh herbs, etc., to taste. Simply pour the cooked variation of your choice over the cooked omelet.

> 4 tbsp. (60 mL) butter
>
> 3 tbsp. (50 mL) flour
>
> 3/4 cup (190 mL) light cream or milk or chicken stock

Melt the butter in a bowl 1 minute at HIGH. Add the flour. Stir to mix. Add the liquid of your choice. Stir to mix. Microwave 2 minutes at HIGH. Stir and microwave at MEDIUM another minute, if necessary, to obtain a creamy sauce. Pour over the cooked omelet.

Creamed Leek Sauce

> 1 leek, the white part and some of the green
>
> 2 tbsp. (30 mL) butter
>
> Salt and pepper to taste
>
> A recipe of Velouté Sauce

Clean the leek, remove a few inches of the green, or leave it all if it has been cut at the shop. Slice thinly. Melt the butter in a bowl 1 minute at HIGH. Stir in the leek, salt and pepper to taste. Microwave 2 minutes at MEDIUM-HIGH. Add to the Velouté Sauce. Stir to mix. Taste for seasoning. Pour over the 2 or 4-egg omelet.

Florentine Spinach Filling *(photo opposite page 41 bottom)*

> A bag or 1 lb (500 g) fresh spinach
>
> A pinch of freshly grated nutmeg
>
> Salt and pepper to taste
>
> A recipe of Velouté Sauce

Wash spinach under cold running water. Place in a dish. Microwave at HIGH 2 to 3 minutes, stirring after 2 minutes, some spinach may take only 2 minutes to cook. Drain well in a sieve, reserving the liquid. Add enough light cream to it to obtain the 3/4 cup (190 mL) of liquid required to prepare the Velouté Sauce. Microwave 3 minutes at MEDIUM. Season to taste. Stir well, add the well drained, cooked spinach. Mix well. If necessary to warm up, microwave 2 minutes at MEDIUM. Pour over the cooked omelet.

Sauces to Serve with Pasta

Italian Vegetable Spaghetti Sauce

There are few meatless spaghetti sauces. This is a very tasty one which may be prepared with oil or melted bacon fat preferably to other fat.

8 oz (250 g) spaghetti

1/2 cup (125 mL) olive or vegetable oil

2 medium carrots, grated

2 large onions, sliced thin

2 medium leeks, sliced

1 28-oz (796 mL) can of tomatoes

1 tbsp. (15 mL) sugar

1 tsp. (5 mL) salt

1 tbsp. (15 mL) oregano or savory

Microwave the spaghetti according to the Pasta Cooking Chart. There may be slight variations in the cooking time depending on the brand of pasta used. Stir and check doneness.
Microwave the oil 3 minutes at HIGH in an 8-cup (2 L) baking dish. Add the vegetables, the tomatoes, sugar, salt and herbs. Mix thoroughly. Cover and microwave 15 minutes at HIGH. Pour as a sauce over the spaghetti and serve.

Spaghetti Sauce

You will make this spaghetti sauce in no more than twelve minutes. Sometimes, before the sauce is set aside to stand, I add 1 cup (250 mL) diced cheese of one kind or a mixture. The heat of the sauce will melt the cheese.

8 oz (250 g) spaghetti

8 oz (250 g) minced beef or pork

1 large onion, chopped

1/2 cup (125 mL) diced celery with leaves

1 carrot, grated (optional)

1 tsp. (5 mL) basil

1 tsp. (5 mL) savory

1 19-oz (540 mL) can tomatoes

1 tsp. (5 mL) salt

1 tsp. (5 mL) sugar

1/2 tsp. (2 mL) fresh ground pepper

Microwave the spaghetti according to the Pasta Cooking Chart. Place in a baking dish the minced beef or pork, break it up with a fork, add the onion, celery, carrot, basil and savory. Mix together and microwave, uncovered, 8 minutes at HIGH, stirring 2 or 3 times. Add the remaining ingredients. Mix thoroughly and microwave 4 minutes at HIGH. Let stand, covered, 10 minutes. Serve.

Year-round Tomato Sauce *(photo : front cover)*

A sauce for all seasons. I would add, for all emergencies. Equally interesting made with fresh or canned tomatoes. Freezes well, but should be thawed out slowly. I defrost mine on the kitchen counter overnight, on folded towelling. When in a hurry, thaw out in the DEFROST cycle of your microwave oven.

1/4 cup (60 mL) olive or vegetable oil

1 large onion, finely chopped

1 garlic clove, finely chopped

1 large 28-oz (796 mL) can tomatoes *or*
   6 fresh tomatoes, peeled and diced

1 5½-oz (156 mL) can tomato paste

1 bay leaf

1/2 tsp. (2 mL) thyme

1 tsp. (5 mL) basil or oregano

2 tsp. (10 mL) sugar

Place the oil of your choice in a large dish, the ideal size being 6 cups (1.5 mL). Microwave at HIGH 2 minutes.

Add the onion and garlic, stir until well coated with the oil. Microwave 4 minutes at MEDIUM-HIGH, stirring once, the onion should be tender but not browned. Add the remaining ingredients. Stir to mix well. Microwave at MEDIUM-HIGH 8 to 10 minutes, stirring after 5 minutes of cooking. There is enough sauce to serve with 8 ounces (250 g) of cooked pasta of your choice.

Fresh Tomato Sauce for Pasta *(photo opposite page 16)*

I can never resist making this super fresh tomato sauce with the first tomatoes in my garden. I like to pour the sauce over delicate cooked pasta, like fine noodles or little stars.

3 large ripe unpeeled tomatoes	1 tbsp. (15 mL) basil
1 tbsp. (15 mL) butter or olive oil	2 cups (500 mL) fine noodles or star pasta
1 tsp. (5 mL) sugar	Salt to taste

Cut the unpeeled mashed tomatoes into 6 to 8 pieces. Place in a Pyrex or Corning dish. Microwave at HIGH 8 to 10 minutes or until sauce has thickened, stirring twice during the cooking period. The texture should be like that of a thick but creamy sauce. Add the remaining ingredients, except the pasta and salt. Stir until creamy.
Microwave the fine noodles or star pasta according to Pasta Cooking Chart. Add the tomato sauce and salt. Stir well and serve or warm up at MEDIUM for 3 or 4 minutes.

The Simplest of All Fresh Tomato Sauces

Not only the simplest, but one of the best, quick and easy sauces. I sometimes use it mixed gently with 2 cups (500 mL) of cooked brown rice, or to serve as a main dish with a bowl of grated cheese, or to add to a roasted meat gravy, or with a roast of veal.

1½ to 2 cups (375 to 500 mL) ripe, unpeeled tomatoes, thickly sliced	1 tsp. (5 mL) sugar
1 tbsp. (15 mL) butter or olive oil	1/2 tsp. (2 mL) basil or oregano or thyme

Place the tomatoes in a dish, microwave at HIGH 2 to 4 minutes, stirring after 2 minutes. When ready, the tomatoes should have a nice, creamy texture, stir in the remaining ingredients until the mixture is light and smooth. This very simple, tasty sauce is at its best when cooked and served over small pasta. I learned how to make this sauce in the south of France. They serve it over pasta, rice, or to top poached or fried fish.
In the summer, when basil is at its best in the garden, place a few stems in a jar, setting it on the table with a pair of scissors. Each one cuts the fresh basil to taste on top of the cooked noodles when ready to eat. Super!

Chicken Liver Spaghetti Sauce

A speciality of Verona, Italy, one of the famous Italian pasta sauces, that can be prepared in 20 minutes and turns out perfectly. Fresh tomatoes are not always available and sometimes quite costly. I believe the quality of the sauce is worth the expense.

2 tbsp. (30 mL) butter
1 lb (500 g) chicken livers, diced
2 tbsp. (30 mL) butter
2 garlic cloves, chopped fine
2 large onions, chopped fine
1/2 cup (125 mL) fresh mushrooms, sliced
1 tsp. (5 mL) salt
1/2 tsp. (2 mL) pepper

1/2 tsp. (2 mL) dry mustard
2 fresh tomatoes, peeled and diced
1 tbsp. (15 mL) flour
3 tbsp. (50 mL) tomato paste
1 cup (250 mL) undiluted canned consommé
1 tsp. (5 mL) basil
1/2 tsp. (2 mL) rosemary or marjoram

Place the first 2 tablespoons (30 mL) butter in a 4-cup (1 L) microwave-safe dish. Microwave at HIGH 2 minutes. Add the diced chicken livers. Stir well. Microwave at HIGH 3 minutes, stirring once. Remove the livers from the dish.
Melt the second 2 tablespoons (30 mL) butter in the same dish 2 minutes at HIGH; add the garlic and onions, microwave at HIGH 4 minutes. Stir and add the mushrooms. Mix well and microwave 1 minute at HIGH. Add the salt, pepper and dry mustard. Stir well, add the diced tomatoes, stir again. Microwave at HIGH 4 minutes.
Stir together the tomato paste and the flour. Add to the tomato mixture, stir in the consommé, basil and rosemary or marjoram. Microwave at HIGH 4 minutes, stirring once.
This sauce will keep 4 to 6 days refrigerated, covered. Warm up at MEDIUM, as needed. The time varies according to the quantity.
This sauce freezes very well and may be kept frozen for 3 to 4 months. When you wish to use it, just place frozen in the microwave, warm up at MEDIUM-HIGH, uncovered, until hot.

Sienna Sauce

A very good vegetarian type of pasta sauce. It will keep 4 to 6 days refrigerated, 2 to 3 months frozen.*

1/2 cup (125 mL) vegetable oil
2 medium-sized carrots, grated
2 large onions, chopped fine
2 medium-sized leeks, thinly sliced

1 large 28-oz (796 mL) can tomatoes
2 tsp. (10 mL) sugar
1 tsp. (5 mL) salt

Place the oil in a 6-cup (1.5 mL) dish. Microwave at HIGH 2 minutes. Add the remaining ingredients, stir well. Microwave 15 minutes at MEDIUM-HIGH.
Serve over cooked pasta or rice.

When frozen, if you wish to use only small quantities at a time, divide the cooked sauce into 2 or 3 containers and freeze.

Simone's Eggplant Sauce

My friend Simone always said she could not cook, but every time she did, the result was perfect and delicious, including this sauce that can be served over rice or noodles, or to top a casserole, or with small pasta. It is superb poured over fried fillets of fish.

1 medium eggplant, peeled and diced	1 19-oz (540 mL) can tomatoes
2 tbsp. (30 mL) bacon fat or oil	1 tsp. (5 mL) salt
1 large garlic clove, chopped fine	1/4 tsp. (1 mL) pepper
1 medium or large green pepper, diced	1 tsp. (5 mL) sugar
1 tsp. (5 mL) sweet basil	3 cups (750 mL) elbow macaroni, cooked

Soak the eggplant in cold water for 10 minutes, then drain it thoroughly. Place the bacon fat or oil in a dish, microwave 2 minutes at HIGH. Add the garlic, green pepper and basil. Microwave 3 minutes at MEDIUM-HIGH, stir and add the tomatoes, salt, pepper and sugar, stir and add the well-drained eggplant. Stir and microwave 10 minutes at MEDIUM-HIGH.
Add the elbow macaroni, stir well and microwave according to instructions in Pasta Cooking Chart. Serve with a bowl of grated cheese of your choice.

Tomato Sauce "Bonne Santé"
Microwave and Convection

This tasty and colorful sauce could also be called Summer Delight because it is at its best when gardens are filled with fresh vegetables.

1 10-oz (384 g) bag fresh spinach	4 large tomatoes
1/4 cup (60 mL) chives, chopped fine or 4 green onions, diced	2 tbsp. (30 mL) butter
1 egg, lightly beaten	Salt and pepper to taste
1/2 cup (125 mL) grated Cheddar*	

Wash the spinach, place in a bowl, microwave 2 minutes at HIGH. Pour into sieve, press with a spoon to remove excess water. When well drained, chop with two knives. Salt and pepper to taste, add the chives or green onions. Mix well, microwave at MEDIUM 2 minutes. Beat the egg with the cheese. Mix thoroughly.
Cut tops of tomatoes, hollow out, squeeze each tomato gently to remove some of the seeds. Sprinkle a little sugar into each tomato. Dice the pulp from inside the tomatoes and add to the spinach mixture. Replace tops removed from the tomatoes.
Preheat the convection part of your microwave oven 10 minutes at 375°F. (190°C). Place tomatoes on a plate, bake 20 to 25 minutes according to their size. Serve with cooked pasta of your choice, microwaved according to basic instructions in Pasta Cooking Chart, and a bowl of grated cheese. Very good, light vegetarian dish.

* A mild or strong cheese can be used.

Quiche lorraine (p. 68) →

Helpful tips in Microwave Cooking

← Top : Pasta Salad "à la Capri" (p. 48)
← Bottom : Summer Spaghetti

Getting to Know You is Loving You

This seems the perfect theme to apply to the Microwave Oven.

As you get to know your microwave better, you become more and more aware of the wonderful flexibility it gives your cooking and meal planning. It also provides far more than just cooking food more quickly, preparation time is also shortened by eliminating unnecessary steps and dishes, hence a saving in clean-up time. For example, a 4-cup (1 L) measure can often be used to measure, mix and cook ingredients.

When entering your kitchen, before beginning to cook, reflect for a moment and think of what can be microwaved to shorten and ease the work. Something to defrost, fat to melt, syrup to make, topping to prepare, hard butter to soften, a sauce to make without constant stirring, and so on.

May the following ideas from my kitchen help you save time and enjoy cooking with your Microwave.

A Few Steps to Insure Good Defrosting for Most Foods

At two-thirds of the way through the total Defrost Cycle, stop the microwave. Let rest in the oven for a period of time. The amount of resting time needed for the temperature to equalize is based on the weight of the product:

1 - 2 lb (500 - 1000 g)	3 minutes standing time in oven after defrosting
3 - 5 lb (1.5 - 2.25 kg)	5 minutes standing time in oven after defrosting
5 - 7 lb (2.25 - 3.5 kg)	10 minutes standing time in oven after defrosting
7 lb (3.5 kg) or more	15 minutes standing time in oven after defrosting

If food is not completely thawed out, return it to the microwave at Defrost for a minute or two, as needed.

* **Butter or Cream Cheese, To Soften:** Place stick or 1/2 cup of butter or cream cheese on serving plate. Microwave 5 seconds at HIGH. Let stand 15 seconds. If necessary, repeat this timing until the required softness is reached.

* **Butter or Other Fat, To Melt:** Place required butter or other fat in a glass dish or measuring cup. Microwave, uncovered, from 30 seconds to 2 minutes at HIGH, depending on quantity and temperature of fat.

* **Butter, Garlic:** Microwave 1 cup (250 mL) butter or margarine with 3 garlic cloves, peeled and split in two, 3 minutes at MEDIUM-HIGH. Let stand 18 minutes, remove garlic. Pour butter into glass jar. Cover, refrigerate. It will keep for months. When needed for buttering bread, seasoning steak or flavoring chicken, just take out what you need.

Whipped Butter

As this butter keeps for a month, refrigerated, do a pound (500 g) at a time. To obtain super extra Whipped Butter, use unsalted butter.

Place a pound (500 g) of unsalted butter in freezer for 12 to 24 hours. Unwrap it, place in a bowl, microwave 1 minute at HIGH, let stand 1 minute, by which time the butter should be soft. If not, heat another 30 seconds. Then beat with a wire whisk or a hand beater until creamy. Place in a bowl, making large swirls on top, or in a wide-mouthed jar, refrigerate, covered. Even cold it will melt instantly on hot pancakes or waffles or toast.

* **Brown Sugar, To Soften:** To soften brown sugar that has hardened, place it on a glass dish with a slice of fresh bread or a piece of apple, cover and microwave at HIGH 30 seconds, for 1 cup (250 mL).

A Few Notes on Honey

Honey has been a natural food and sweetening ingredient for thousands of years. It is easier to digest than sugar, it gives a quick lift when you are tired. Fold a spoonful of honey into whipped cream for a rich flavor.
Add it to lemon or orange juice to make a drink or to glaze a slice of ham or chicken legs, then microwave. Delicious!
Do not store honey in the refrigerator. Keep it in a dark cupboard.
1 tablespoon of honey = 1 oz
Dip spoon into hot water before measuring honey. It will then slip off the spoon quite easily.

Lemon Honey

Interesting topping for hot rolls or toast of your choice.
Add the juice and grated rind of 1 lemon to 1 cup (250 mL) honey. Microwave in glass jug or small bowl 1 minute at HIGH. Stir for a few seconds. Let stand at room temperature (prepare the night before, to serve at breakfast). It will keep 4 to 6 weeks refrigerated.

* **Honey, To Clarify:** If honey has turned to sugar, uncover jar, microwave 30 seconds to 1 minute at HIGH, depending on quantity of honey. Remove from oven as soon as liquified.

* **Heating Liquid Honey or Corn Syrup or Maple Syrup:** Remove metal cap from bottle, microwave, uncovered, 30 to 45 seconds at HIGH for a 13-oz bottle or until bubbles appear. A pitcher can also be used.

* **Prunes, To Soften or Pit:** Place prunes in glass bowl or jar, barely cover with leftover tea or coffee or part water, part orange juice. If you so wish, add 1 star anise or 1 stick cinnamon or 2 cloves or the grated rind of an orange or lemon. Microwave, uncovered, 8 minutes at MEDIUM. Let stand 10 minutes. Warm pitted prunes to serve over your hot cereal. They will keep 4 to 5 weeks refrigerated, covered, in their liquid.

* **Apricots, To Rehydrate:** To make jam or cake filling, we often have to soak these for a few hours. In the microwave oven, simply put the needed quantity of apricots in a bowl with just enough water or other liquid of your choice to barely cover them. Heat 6 minutes at MEDIUM, let stand 3 to 5 minutes.

Try the following:

A Golden Mousse: Soften the apricots with orange juice. Pour into a blender. Blend to a puree. Beat 2 egg whites, fold into puree **or**

Make a Tasty Cake Filling: Soften the apricots with cream. Blend with a small spoonful of butter. Cool and use.

Make a Creamy Cake Topping: Proceed as for Cake Filling. Refrigerate overnight, or place 1 hour in freezer. Fold in whipped cream to taste.

* Ice Cream, To Soften: Microwave at WARM 1 to 2 minutes depending on quantity. Check.

* Raisins, To Soften: When your recipe calls for this, pour a little water over raisins. Microwave, uncovered, 3 minutes at MEDIUM. Let stand 2 minutes, drain and use.

To Make Madeira Raisins to Serve with Curry: Proceed as above, pouring 1/4 cup (60 mL) of dry or sweet Madeira instead of water over 1 cup (250 mL) Muscatel raisins. Microwave 3 minutes at MEDIUM, let stand 2 minutes. Serve hot or cold, but do not drain.

* Dehydrated Fruit, To Soften: Place the fruit in a bowl and sprinkle with water. Cover and microwave at MEDIUM 30 to 45 seconds.

* Chocolate, To Melt: Melt the 1-oz (28 g) squares of unsweetened or semi-sweet chocolate in their waxed paper wrappers, seam side up, on a plate 1 minute at MEDIUM. Scrape chocolate from paper with a rubber spatula. The measurements are then very accurate as no chocolate is lost on the sides of the pan — and there's no pan to wash.

Chocolate Substitutes

3 tbsp. (50 mL) cocoa + 1 tbsp. (15 mL) butter = 1 square or 1 oz (28 g) unsweetened chocolate
3 tbsp. (50 mL) cocoa + 1 tbsp. (15 mL) butter + 1½ tsp. (7 mL) sugar = 1 square or 1 oz (28 oz) sweet chocolate.

Baking Powder Substitute

If you find yourself out of baking powder when ready to use it, replace with the following:
Mix together:

2 tsp. (10 mL) cream of tartar

1 tsp. (5 mL) baking soda

1/4 tsp. (2 mL) salt

Mix well and use for each 2 cups (500 mL) of flour called for in your recipe.

* **Almonds, Toasted:** To toast 1 cup (250 mL) of blanched whole, slivered or halved almonds or other types of nuts, simply spread them on a plate. Microwave 2 or 3 minutes at MEDIUM-HIGH, stirring every minute so they will brown evenly. Let stand 2 minutes as they continue browning. Stir again. Handy to have on hand to sprinkle on fish, vegetables or desserts.

* **Almonds, To Remove Brown Skins:** Place almonds in a bowl, cover with water, microwave at HIGH in boiling water 30 seconds to 1 minute. Cool and rub between your fingers to remove skins.

* **Dried Fruits, To Plump:** When a recipe (even one baked the conventional way) calls for dried fruits and nuts to be soaked 12 to 24 hours with a quantity of rum or brandy, use same quantity of fruits, nuts and rum or brandy. Mix in a large bowl. Microwave 5 minutes, covered, at MEDIUM. No amount of ordinary cooking can make them as moist or as tasty. I use this with all my favorite festive fruitcakes.

* **Liquor to Flame a Dessert, To Heat:** Microwave the liquor called for in a glass container 15 to 30 seconds at HIGH.

* **Oranges, Lemons or Limes, To Get More Juice:** Place fruits, one at a time, for 30 seconds at MEDIUM in microwave oven before squeezing.

* **Orange and Lemon Rind, To Dry:** Spread the rind on a plate. Microwave 30 seconds to 1 minute at HIGH, stirring once.

* **Peaches, To Peel:** Microwave peaches 15 to 20 seconds at MEDIUM, depending on their size, let stand 10 minutes and peel.

* **Bread Cubes or Breadcrumbs:** Microwave 2 cups (500 mL) bread cubes or breadcrumbs in a shallow glass dish 2 to 3 minutes at HIGH, stirring a few times.

* **Potato Chips or Crackers, To Refresh:** Place soggy potato chips or crackers in a plate and microwave about 45 seconds to 1 minute at MEDIUM-HIGH. Let stand 1 minute to crisp. It's nice to serve warm, crispy crackers with your soup.

* **Tea or Coffee Leftover:** To reheat, place required quantity in cup, microwave 1 minute at HIGH.

* **Ketchup, Leftover:** Turn into a sauce. Remove metal cap from bottle, add a spoonful or two of leftover red wine or cream or orange juice or Madeira, and a square of butter. Microwave 2 to 3 minutes at MEDIUM, depending on quantity. Add to brown sauce or spaghetti sauce or serve over rice.

* **Baby Bottles, To Warm:** Fill a 4-oz (125 mL) or 8-oz (250 mL) bottle or plastic nurser with milk. Invert nipple and screw cap on loosely. Microwave at MEDIUM 45 seconds for a 4-oz (125 mL) bottle, 1 minute 20 seconds for an 8-oz (250 mL) bottle. Turn nipple to outside, tighten cap and shake vigorously. Test temperature on wrist.

* **Baby Food, To Warm:** Strained or junior foods can be heated in their containers, but first always remember to remove cap. (Never microwave a sealed or capped jar). For 3½ to 7¾-oz (98 - 228 mL) containers, microwave individually from 30 to 45 seconds at MEDIUM. Three jars heated together, placed in a circle, will take 1 minute to 1 minute 30 seconds.

* **Cooking Odor, To Remove:** To remove any cooking odor from oven, mix together in a small bowl the juice and rind of a lemon with a little water. Microwave at HIGH 5 minutes, then wipe inside of microwave oven with a damp cloth.

How to Dry Herbs in the Microwave

For many years I have successfully dried herbs from my garden. They retain their flavor and color.

For All Fresh Herbs

Tarragon, basil, marjoram, savory, sage, thyme, mint, etc., all come out with flying colors.
Separate the leaves from the stem. Spread the leaves on a sheet of paper towelling. Cover the leaves with another sheet of paper and microwave about 1 minute at HIGH. Turn over, if bottom sheet is damp, microwave 40 to 50 seconds at HIGH. When dried, pour into a bowl and let them cool. Bottle and cover. They will keep in perfect condition for a full year.
Herbs all have different texture, thickness and moistness, which explains why no absolutely exact time applies to them all. After drying a few, you will understand the easy process.

General Index

NOTES

NOTES

NOTES

NOTES

NOTES

Printed by
PAYETTE & SIMMS INC.
in March, 1987
at Saint-Lambert, Qué.